The
Spiritual Journey
of a Misfit

Books by Francis Dorff, O. Praem.

The Art of Passingover:
An Invitation to Living Creatively

The Journey from Misery to Ministry:
Living Creatively in a Broken World

Simply SoulStirring:
Writing as a Meditative Practice

We are One in the Spirit:
Homilies Facing Death
(with Joseph Dorff, O. Praem.)

The Rabbi's Gift:
An Untold Story

Soul Songs to God:
A Haiku Psalter

Last Night I Died:
Poems from Retirement

The Flowering of the TreeCross:
An Experience in LifeProcess Meditating

The Spiritual Journey of a Misfit

A Personal Pilgrimage
Francis Dorff, O. Praem.

SUNSTONE PRESS
SANTA FE

© 2015 by Francis Dorff, O. Praem.
All Rights Reserved.
No part of this book may be reproduced in any form or by any electronic or mechanical means including information storage and retrieval systems without permission in writing from the publisher, except by a reviewer who may quote brief passages in a review.

Sunstone books may be purchased for educational, business, or sales promotional use. For information please write: Special Markets Department, Sunstone Press, P.O. Box 2321, Santa Fe, New Mexico 87504-2321.

Book and cover design › Vicki Ahl
Body typeface › Adobe Caslon Pro
Printed on acid-free paper
∞
eBook 978-1-61139-432-0

Library of Congress Cataloging-in-Publication Data

Names: Dorff, Francis.
Title: The spiritual journey of a misfit : a personal pilgrimage / by Francis
 Dorff, O. Praem.
Description: Santa Fe : Sunstone Press, 2016.
Identifiers: LCCN 2015036233 | ISBN 9781632930927 (softcover : alk. paper)
Subjects: LCSH: Dorff, Francis. | Catholic Church--United
 States--Clergy--Biography. | Priests--United States--Biography.
Classification: LCC BX4705.D63755 A3 2016 | DDC 271/.1902--dc23
LC record available at http://lccn.loc.gov/2015036233

SUNSTONE PRESS IS COMMITTED TO MINIMIZING OUR ENVIRONMENTAL IMPACT ON THE PLANET. THE PAPER USED IN THIS BOOK IS FROM RESPONSIBLY MANAGED FORESTS. OUR PRINTER HAS RECEIVED CHAIN OF CUSTODY (COC) CERTIFICATION FROM: THE FOREST STEWARDSHIP COUNCIL™ (FSC®), PROGRAMME FOR THE ENDORSEMENT OF FOREST CERTIFICATION™ (PEFC™), AND THE SUSTAINABLE FORESTRY INITIATIVE® (SFI®).
THE FSC® COUNCIL IS A NON-PROFIT ORGANIZATION, PROMOTING THE ENVIRONMENTALLY APPROPRIATE, SOCIALLY BENEFICIAL AND ECONOMICALLY VIABLE MANAGEMENT OF THE WORLD'S FORESTS. FSC® CERTIFICATION IS RECOGNIZED INTERNATIONALLY AS A RIGOROUS ENVIRONMENTAL AND SOCIAL STANDARD FOR RESPONSIBLE FOREST MANAGEMENT.

WWW.SUNSTONEPRESS.COM
SUNSTONE PRESS / POST OFFICE BOX 2321 / SANTA FE, NM 87504-2321 /USA
(505) 988-4418 / ORDERS ONLY (800) 243-5644 / FAX (505) 988-1025

To celebrate the gift of my Diamond Jubilee of being alive
and my Golden Jubilee of being a Norbertine priest,
I have written these memoirs in praise and thanks to God
and dedicate them to my sister and brother misfits all over the world
that they may be given the courage
to remain faithful to their calling.

With heartfelt thanks to:

Abbot Joel P. Garner, O.Praem., for giving me the space and time in which to write;

Meg Ashcroft, O.Praem. Obl., for her dedicated editing of this manuscript;

Sally Severino, MD, for encouraging me to have this manuscript published; and

Amy Gardner, PhD, for her careful reading of this manuscript and her many thoughtful suggestions for improving it.

Contents

Invocation

1 Talking to My Self / 9
2 Living with a Restless Heart / 14
3 An Image of Who I Am / 25
4 A Most Untimely Birth / 37
5 Two Perennial Questions / 42
6 Leaving the World / 46
7 Changing My Name / 55
8 Being a Stranger in a Strange Land / 62
9 Experiencing a Communal Change of Heart / 72
10 Living from the Easter Side / 78
11 Who Closed the Classroom Door? / 88
12 Letting My Life Be Wise / 94
13 Living in the In-Between / 103
14 The Strange Affair / 112
15 Getting it All Together / 121
16 Rebuilding the Church / 128
17 In the Shadow of Mother Church / 140
18 Becoming a Judeo-Christian / 152
19 Becoming a Catacomb Christian / 163
20 Becoming an Anonymous Priest / 171
21 Seeking Wisdom Side-by-Side / 180
22 Getting to Know My Soul / 187
23 Becoming a Hermit Without a Permit / 201
24 Playing Hide-and-Seek with God / 208
25 A Timely Death / 217

Invocation

Psalm 139

From my mother's womb
You have loved me into life
and known my wonder.
    —Soul Songs to God: A Haiku Psalter

1

Talking to My Self

Now why should I tell you my story? You know it through and through. You know it better than I do. From my mother's womb you've been with me every step of the way. Even when I'm not with you, you're always with me. If you hadn't been with me all along, who would I be? If you weren't always present to me, how would I be present to my self? I'd have no story to tell and no one to tell it to. I don't have to tell you that. That's what your presence keeps telling me. Now, if I don't have to tell you that, I certainly don't have to tell you my story. So why do you keep prompting me to tell you my story?

Besides, whenever I get caught talking to you, it gets me into all kinds of trouble. People think I'm crazy. They think I'm talking to myself.

In a sense, I guess they're right. I *am* talking to my Self, but not in the way they mean it. They seem to think that what they see is all there is to me. So they can't really see me at all. And if they can't see me, they certainly can't see you. If they ever did think that you existed, they think it must have been "once upon a time." Now they think that you've gotten lost somewhere in the Middle Ages or died when we reached the Age of Reason.

So all they can see is me standing alone, as I often do. If they even suspect that I'm talking to you in my solitude, they avoid me like the plague. Yet, deep down, my whole life is nothing if it's not a soliloquy.

It's not as though I haven't tried to speak to them from within my relationship with you—especially more recently. But when I do, you should see them. They blush with embarrassment; or their eyes glaze over; or there's an awkward pause in the conversation; or they cough as though I had just polluted the atmosphere. They then go back to talking about their job, or their ministry, or, God help us, the bishop, or, God help us again, the Green Bay Packers.

Even my faculty colleagues and the psychologists who were on staff with me would act that way. What's more, so would my monastic confreres in the Order of Prémontré. And we're part of a tradition that has been committed to embodying the apostolic ideal of "being of one mind and one heart on the journey into God" for close to nine hundred years now. How we can ever be of one mind and one heart without telling one another what's going on within us has always been a mystery to me. But there you have it. You know what I mean.

It can be even more awkward if the person I'm trying to speak heart-to-heart with has been reading everything the experts have to say in the field of psychology. In that case, they're often so busy collecting data that they can't even hear what you're saying within them. So how can they possibly hear me when I'm trying to tell them what you're saying within *me*? I honestly don't think they can. They're like the girl I took to the arboretum on one of my first dates. I was awestruck when I first caught sight of a cedar of Lebanon off in the distance. "Look at that magnificent tree!" I exclaimed.

"Yes," she replied. "It reminds me of what the poet said so well:

"Poems are made by fools like me,
But only God can make a tree."

I immediately took a mental note: "This is my last date with her."

I suspect she may have returned the compliment, too, since I never saw her again. She probably thought I was crazy, or, as we would say as teenagers in the forties, "weird."

If so, she wouldn't be the last date to think that about me. I know, because a couple of my dates felt obliged to tell me so face to face. That doesn't make for a pleasant evening. I don't have to tell you that.

Later on, some of my colleagues in philosophy and theology would go in a much more sophisticated direction with my attempts to tell them what you were stirring up within me. With minor variations on this theme, they'd say something like, "Well, with regard to that," (here they often cleared their throat, or took the pipe out of their mouth and exhaled thoughtfully), "on one hand, with Heidegger, you could argue that.... On the other hand, Thomas Aquinas would argue.... Or, you *could* take Whitehead's position and argue...." These are just a few of the options they would outline in painstaking detail. This laid the foundation for an argument or two behind which we both could safely hide. Then I'd forget that I hadn't wanted to argue. I'd wanted to share with them what you were stirring up within me. So much for that.

Even though I understood this academic approach a bit better, at times it could be just as painful for me as talking about the Green Bay Packers.

But I don't really blame my colleagues for relating to me in this way. For the most part, this was the way in which we were all educated, no matter where we were educated. It was the *lingua franca* of academe. We all spoke it quite fluently; and I spoke it more fluently than most. That's *all* we spoke, too, unless we began to talk college politics, and that could be very ugly.

All the while you were trying to let our lives teach us a second language. As you know, learning that language was a slow painful process for me. It took me about twenty-five years.

No matter how slow and painful the process was, though, it was worth it. I'm so happy to be bilingual now.

So, if you already know my story, and if it's of precious little interest to others, why do you keep prompting me to tell it to you? You know I can no longer tell it as though I'm an outsider to it. I'm *not* an outsider to it. Together with you, I'm *the* insider of my story. Nobody else has ever experienced it in the way I experience it. No one has ever experienced it from the inside out. Without my presence within it, my whole story is personally meaningless. I know that from the many *curricula vitae* I've written for different job applications. At the time I wrote them, I found them "interesting" and even somewhat flattering. Now, they read like an obituary. What's worse, the obituary is mine!

My real story just isn't there. It lies in the silent, blank spaces between and beneath these lifeless litanies of outside facts. When I honor that empty space, these facts have a way of coming to life again for me. They start dancing around in the desert like the prophet Ezekiel's famous "dry bones." Some of the most creative things in my life have come from that dance. I don't have to tell you that.

Of course, the outside facts of my life are historically true. It's just that they're by no means the whole story. That's because my story isn't a scrapbook of lifeless photos. It's a moving picture that has moved me, and continues to move me, very deeply. My story isn't just a history. It's a unique history of a mystery unfolding from the inside out, and it isn't over yet. As I look at it, this is true of every person I know. Each one of us is a mystery with an open-ended history.

I really marvel at the history of my mystery. At seventy-five years old, I'm *still* a mystery to myself! I *still* haven't figured out the story I'm living. I *still* haven't "pieced it all together." I don't remember where it all began. And I don't really know how it's going to end. That leaves me living a mystery story that, no matter how hard I might try, I just can't put down.

Of course, I tend to forget this in my arrogantly naïve "self-made man" moments. But deep down, I not only know it; I *delight* in it. It's a constant source of wonder to me. That's the story I'd really like to tell you if I could. It's the inside story that you keep telling me. But, as I say, you know this story better that I do. So why should I bother telling it to you?

My sister-in-law, Mary, used to say that when her twelve children would talk about their childhood, she would begin to wonder whether or not she had been there at the time. Of course, she was there. But her children were telling the story from the inside out, and every one of them had a uniquely personal version of it. On the one hand, that's very rich. On the other hand, it can make you wonder whether you were there.

But, wait a minute! Maybe you want me to tell my story to you anyway, not so that *you* can hear it, but so that *I* can hear it again and be thankful.

You know, that would make very good sense to me. My story comes to me one memory, dream, or reflection at a time, like isolated drops of rain. That's not how I live it, though. I live it as a deeply flowing river of meaning in which you and I are swimming. The way that river is flowing feels and looks very different to me at different times in my life. So it makes perfectly good sense to me that you might want to hear how it looks to me right *now*. It's like the storyteller I knew who'd sometimes begin telling a story by saying, "Now I want you to be very quiet while I tell this story, because I really want to hear what I'm saying."

But maybe that's not it at all. Maybe, deep down, *you're* the one who wants to tell my story; and you want to tell it to *me*. Maybe, in my old age, you want to give me the chance to hear it all over again, as if for the first time.

I think that might *really* be what you have in mind. I know from experience that that's how you work. You tell me my story so that I may re-member it from the inside out. That way, if others overhear it, that's not all they hear. They begin to hear their own story resonating behind your words and they start to wonder where in the world *that's* coming from.

You and I know full well where it's coming from. It's coming from you. That's how you work. You have a way of telling a story so that everyone thinks it's just like his or hers and we all wind up swimming together in the same river. That's the marvelous kind of storyteller you are.

Well, if you really want to tell me my story again, go for it. I'll be more than happy to listen to you telling it and to write it down as faithfully as I can. Even though I know parts of your present version of it may be embarrassing for me, that doesn't bother me. I've been embarrassed before. Besides, I can hardly wait to hear how my story sounds this time around. And if someone else should happen to overhear you telling it and think that I'm just talking to my Self, so be it.

2

Living with a Restless Heart

You have made us for yourself, O Lord,
and our hearts are restless
until they rest in you.

—Augustine of Hippo, *Confessions*

I've always had a restless heart but I never realized just how restless it could actually be until my pulse went up to one hundred and eighty beats a minute and stayed around that for about three weeks.

I found out later that they call this "atrial fibrillation." At the time, I called it "pleurisy." This was the word my mother used to use to cover a multitude of illnesses—everything from "growing pains," to the common cold, to pneumonia, and beyond. All I knew was that I was gasping for breath, my ribs were hurting, I had to sleep sitting up straight to breathe, had very little energy, and could hardly walk. Apart from that, I was fine. So I just kept on teaching.

Since there wasn't a doctor in the house, I asked a nurse at the workshop at which this all began to take my pulse. She tried, but then quietly walked away saying, "I can't pick up a pulse."

It would have been nice had I recognized this incident as the red flag that it really was. Instead, I took it as a sign to start eating cough drops as if they were going out of style.

All of this started shortly after I arrived at the Vallombrosa Retreat House in Menlo Park, California, and discovered that my friend Ira Progoff, with whom I had agreed to lead a very large Intensive Journal Workshop, had been taken to the hospital. That meant that I would have to lead the workshop on my own.

As I opened the first session I could see the great disappointment on the faces of the one hundred or so participants. Here I was, an unknown priest (of all things) from New Mexico (of all places) replacing the celebrated guru-founder of holistic depth psychology whom the participants had paid good money to work with. I couldn't blame them for being disappointed. I would have been disappointed myself. In fact, I was.

As we got started, I could feel that these retreatants were much more familiar with transactional analysis group interaction than they were with the deeply contemplative work that we would be doing. So I spent our first session feeling as though I was trying single-handedly to pull in the reins on a hundred-mule team until they began to realize the direction in which we would be going. Eventually, most of them got it but, that night, my heart got restless.

It wasn't until two weeks later that my Tai Chi teacher noticed that something was seriously wrong with me. Without even trying to take my pulse he could feel the heat coming from my wrist and immediately sent me to the emergency room.

My weeklong stay in Presbyterian Hospital gave me several opportunities to get an insider's view of my restless heart on the monitor. I was amazed. I had no idea that this sort of thing was even possible. In disbelief, I asked the cardiovascular technician, "Is that *my* heart that I'm looking at?"

"Of course it is," she said matter-of-factly, looking at me as though I had just come from Mars. I guess she was so accustomed to looking inside the human heart that it wasn't a big deal for her anymore. But, as a first-timer, it certainly still was a big deal for me.

In any case, the technician didn't hold my naivete against me. She was kind enough to give me the full tour of my heart in glowing Technicolor, including the haunting sound of my heartbeat and blood flow, several different perspectives from within my heart, and a detailed commentary on what was going on there.

Right in the middle of the picture, I could see the valve of my heart trying as hard as it could to keep beating. It looked like a little man dancing frantically to an impossible tempo and unable to keep up. He reminded me of how I must have looked when I was jitterbugging a very long time ago. I really felt sorry for him.

The week in the hospital gave me a lot of time to meditate on the dancing of my frenzied heart. It made me realize how much I had been taking for granted the tremendous gift of my heartbeat. It also made me feel that the televised inside view of my heart in trouble was actually a portrait of how frantically I had been living my life on so many occasions. It was a portrait of my heart in a very big hurry on the way to burnout. I had been living, studying, working, and ministering as though my heart was a one-directional mechanical pump, if there is such a thing, just giving, giving, and giving with hardly any rest or relief. As the car commercial says, I was driven. The problem was, so was my heart.

But the sound and sight of my own heart beating also reminded me that it actually was a marvel of nature: a living, two-stroke muscle with a three-phase pulse, rhythmically receiving, *resting*, and giving; receiving, *resting*, and giving.

There was a lesson for me in this heartbeat and it wasn't just a lesson in physiology—although God knows I was long overdue for a lesson in physiology. It was also a lesson in spirituality. My thoughtful cardiovascular technician had given me much more than she realized.

I began to wonder how someone like me, who believed so deeply in the Incarnation of the God I loved and served, could be so out of touch with my own body. And I was a theologian to boot!

One of my doctors also seemed to be wondering about this. In fact, he seemed to be astounded by how obtuse I was. Evidently, atrial fibrillation isn't all that difficult to detect.
"All you have to do is to look at your shirt pocket moving up and down to see that your heart's beating way too fast," he told me.

He may have been overstating his case a bit, but he made his point very clearly.

Eventually, I had to admit that I really had no excuse, and certainly no theological justification, for being so out of touch with my own body. In my defense, though, I told myself that I'd been brought up in the deeply engrained "brother ass" school of spirituality. In keeping with that, I'd been working hard for over four decades at saddling up "brother ass" with all my "sins of the flesh" and sending him off into the desert in hope that I'd never see him again. Then I could get back to my work of saving the world. Of course, the trouble was, that damned ass just kept coming back. Then I'd have to start all over again. Whether I liked to admit it or not, my ass seemed to be very attached to me.

Even someone as holy as my patron saint, Francis of Assisi, had been brought up in this tradition. Toward the end of his life he too had to apologize to "brother ass" for treating him so thoughtlessly. At least that put me in good company. It wasn't much consolation, though. It in no way justified my being so out of touch with my own body or the violence I had done to myself simply by overlooking him, not to mention trying to exile him into the desert for life.

Besides, I should have known better. I have a better education than Saint Francis did, or at least I used to think I did. The problem was, much of my very sophisticated theological education led me to act as though the Incarnation took place in my head and had precious little to do with my heart and guts, much less my genitals. My body did all he could to break through this disregard but I guess I was so busy saddling him up for the journey into exile that I had a hard time even noticing.

Now and then, though, he would really get my attention. Once, when I was beginning an eight-day solitary retreat, I was hardly able to pray. My body just wouldn't be still. He kept loudly complaining in his typical body language: aches, pains, distractedness, tiredness, and sleepless nights. Finally, I decided to do a dialogue meditation with him to find out what was going on.

Like a long lost friend, my body greeted me warmly. Then he let me know in no uncertain terms that he wanted to be my spiritual director for this retreat. After all, who did I think was kneeling when I was kneeling? And who was doing Tai Chi when I was doing Tai Chi? And who was chanting when I was chanting? And, besides, who did I think I was, calling him, "brother ass"! Talk about getting down to basics!

Anyway, I finally got the point. My body became my retreat master. He led me masterfully in one of the best retreats I've ever made. Who knows? Had I maintained that spiritually cordial relationship with "brother ass," I might never have wound up in the intensive care unit.

As the days dragged by, I began to feel that the bedside manner of one of the doctors who visited me every morning left a bit to be desired. I was very disappointed. He'd pop into the room, take a quick look at my chart, dash over and glance out the window, and—zip—he was out of there.

En route, he might make a quick comment or two about my condition. This routine made it rather difficult for me to get through the whole list of questions I had written down for him in the course of the previous day. So I spoke as fast and I could, and gave it my best shot to catch his attention. I figured this was as good a time as any to begin my lesson in physiology.

One day, he paused for a moment on his way out the door. "I know what kind you are," he said. "You're the kind that asks questions." Then—zip—he disappeared.

He couldn't have been closer to the truth. I *am* the kind that asks questions. I think I began asking questions as soon as I was born. I don't have any hard data on this but I can picture myself turning to my mother as I came out of her womb and asking, "So, Mom, where am I now?"

At any rate, I was an amateur question asker at first. But when I fell in love with philosophy and then with her big sister, theology, I became a real professional asker of questions. Asking questions became a way of life for me.

I remember once when the director of a program in which I was doing spiritual direction called me in on the carpet. He told me to stop asking so many questions in our staff meetings and to limit the ones I asked to the reports on the clients with whom we were working. He didn't want me raising any more "systemic questions" about how the Church, our program, and his administration were operating and what we might be able to do about it.

The next day, I resigned. That's how dedicated I am to asking questions. It's as though my life depends on it. And it really does.

So, the doctor-in-a-hurry really had me pegged. I'm "the kind that asks questions." So I took a mental note: "Make sure this guy doesn't become my regular cardiologist."

As my week in the hospital wore on, I could tell from the look on my cardiologist's face that what, in my ignorance, I'd been taking rather lightly, was getting really serious. So I began trying to persuade God that it would be very bad timing on God's part, and not at all in God's best interest either, to take me now, since my work was not yet finished. I thought that I made my point so insistently and so cogently that I felt for sure that God would have to concede it.

Then one night, I got an unexpected reply. I heard a dream-like voice from within me saying, "Francis, you've got it all wrong."

"I do?" I replied.

"Yes, you do. I don't take you when your work is finished. Your work is finished when I take you."

"Well," I thought to myself, "now that's a fresh way of looking at it!" I felt greatly relieved.

This late night teaching made all the difference in the world in how I faced the rest of the week. It filled me with a deep sense of peace that I couldn't explain. I no longer spent the whole day and half the night trying to tell God what to do. I just put my heart in God's hands in thanksgiving and in praise for the marvel of my being, and kept silently singing variations on "*Que sera, sera.*"

A few days later, my cardiologist burst into the room. He was a smile from ear to ear. "We did it!" he said. "The medicine worked! Your heart is back in sinus rhythm."

All I could say was, "Thank God."

The next day when I visited my technician friend for a final check-up, she treated me to the sight of my heart beating normally. It was a very different picture. My little valve friend had stopped jitterbugging. Thank God. He now looked like a very self-possessed conductor masterfully leading my whole body in an unfinished symphony. I couldn't quite hear what the orchestra was playing but it sounded to me a lot like the moving harmonies of something Shubert composed.

As we looked at this image together, my technician just kept cheering, "What a doctor! What medicine! What a doctor!"

I felt like adding to that chorus, "What music!" but I wasn't sure whether or not she could hear it. All I knew was that I was deeply grateful for the beautiful sight and sound of my heart beating in sinus rhythm. And I was deeply touched by the enthusiastic reception it was getting from these two dedicated heart specialists. It felt like my heart was getting a standing ovation from a most discerning audience that usually reserves this kind of reception for very special performances.

Maybe I have more in common with my cardiologists than I've ever imagined. Just like them, I'm spending my life wondering what makes me tick and marveling all the while at the ticking. I even started taking my pulse as a form of meditation.

I don't know, but it seems to me that I waited awfully long before getting my first inside view of my heart in action. I was already in my late fifties. But whether it came late or not, this image of my heart in action has become a very powerful symbol for me. It symbolizes what my whole life feels like for as long as I can remember. It feels like living with a restless heart. At the heart of my life I clearly hear the heartbeat of a very personalized version of Saint Augustine's classic prayer: "You have made *me* for yourself, O Lord, and *my* heart is restless until it rests in you."

In all honesty, I have to say that this restless heart of mine has not been unadulterated good news for me. At one and the same time, it has been a blessing, a challenge, and a cross.

On the one hand, it has graced me with a heartfelt longing for God and a lifelong love of learning in my search for Wisdom.

> In the secret of my heart, teach me Wisdom.
> In the secret of my heart...
> In the secret of my heart...

On the other hand, no matter where I've been, my restless heart has often made me feel out of place, like some unknown wandering pilgrim. It has obliged me to live with questions that even my best friends wish I wouldn't bother asking. When I do bother asking these questions, my friends hope that I'll be considerate enough to refrain from ever mentioning them again.

My restless heart has made me live simultaneously with both a deep sense of God's mysterious Presence (*"You have made me for yourself, O Lord...."*), *and* an acute awareness of God's painful Absence in my life (*...and my heart is restless until it rests in you"*). All the while, it seems to oblige others to keep asking me in one way or another, *"Where is your God?"*

Just like my physical heart, at times this restless heart of mine can be in perfect sync with the music of Life. I'm deeply delighted when that happens. It's one of my greatest joys.

At other times, however, this restless heart of mine can be frantically beating and totally out of sync with Life's basic rhythm. This is one of my most painful experiences. It's unbelievably awkward and confusing. I don't know why it's happening and I frequently don't have any idea what to do about it. It makes me feel that I've lost my way.

I find that one of the many beauties of this restless heart of mine, though, is that it lets me experience my life from the inside out. If I remain attentive to it, it constantly reminds me that my whole life is a divine gift, not a personal achievement. It gives me a deeply felt sense that what's *really* important to me is not all the things I've said and done in my very rich life as a student, religious, priest, teacher, writer, and spiritual director. What's really important to me is how faithfully I've been following the deepest longing of my restless heart wherever it may lead me. This heartfelt creative fidelity keeps turning me and moving me toward what is really Real. It's the hidden spring of whatever happiness I've ever experienced flowing through my life as a priest.

Another beauty of this restless heart of mine is that it gives me the sense of being a kindred spirit with the many restless seekers of Wisdom whom I've admired, studied, and come to know personally. It lets me meditatively meet with them heart-to-heart. Whether they're living or dead doesn't make any difference. I carry them all in my heart.

My restless heart also teaches me how to minister compassionately to those in transition better than any book I've ever read or any course I've ever taken. This is especially true when, in the times of radical change in which we live, I hear the restless hearts of others leading them to question the real meaning of their work, their relationships, their church, their faith, their culture, their country, their way of life, or their God. Then my heart lets me hear their heartbeat. One ear of my heart listens to their heartbeat while the other one listens to mine. We two have a lot in common. We both are "the kind that asks questions," and who knows where these questions will lead us?

These are just two of the many gifts that my restless heart keeps giving me. I'm immensely grateful for all of them.

It was my restless heart that led me to join the semi-monastic Order of Prémontré at the age of seventeen. I had no idea what this way of life was really all about. I didn't even know what a monastery was. All I knew was that I deeply admired the priests of Prémontré, how dedicatedly they taught me in high school, and how lovingly they seemed to live and serve together. That was more than enough to let me take the leap.

Once I landed, however, I began to learn what this way of life was really all about. I was delighted to discover that the first sentence of our Augustinian Rule of Life reads: "The reason why you come together is to live in harmony and to be of one mind and one heart on your journey into God."

My restless heart resonated right away with this vision of a harmony of head and heart with God and others. It assured me that I was in good company living with the dedicated men of Prémontré and with our spiritual fathers, Augustine of Hippo and Norbert of Xanten. There's no way that I can re-member this initial experience of deep communing and think that it was just a "coincidence." My restless heart tells me otherwise.

What I didn't know at the time, however, was that over the centuries, many of the monastic rules had come to be interpreted as rules for settlers, not for seekers. The brief fifth century rule of the restless-hearted Augustine was no exception. By the time I came along, being faithful to the Rule had gradually come to mean settling down, staying in the same place, doing what you're told without asking any questions, not "rocking the boat," not going out into "the world" too much, trying hard to "pay your dues" in an environment that was designed so that you could never pay your dues, guarding your eyes, subduing your body, keeping your nose to the grindstone until the grindstone finally gives up; and dying with your boots on.

Even as a young man, I wasn't all that fond of the notion of "dying with your boots on" but I didn't question this interpretation of the Rule at all. What did I know? I thought that this was the way they'd been doing things around here for over eight hundred years and that's what I came to the monastery to learn. So, if they raised the bar, I figured it was my job to jump over it. I got pretty good at doing that, too. This probably made me look like a promising candidate for the consecrated life and the priesthood.

However, as I got a little older and got more in touch with my restless heart, I began to experience Augustine's restless heart as a mirror of my own. I then began to realize that, even though there wasn't much room for seekers or questioners in our well-established interpretation of the Rule, Augustine had originally written his Rule of Life for those who were "lovers of spiritual beauty" and passionate seekers of the truth just as he was.

I also began to realize that being faithful to Augustine's Rule of Life takes a very different form for settlers than it does for seekers. I began to learn from painful experience that part of the "dues" that I would have to keep paying for living with a restless heart would be to be perceived as someone who just couldn't settle down, and didn't quite fit in. As my life as a solemnly-vowed Norbertine priest began to unfold a little more, it became very clear to me that being faithful to my restless heart would involve changing, and changing often, no matter what the cost would be. As a seeker, this is the way I'm being called to live my life and to live our Rule of Life. It's just how it is with me, and how it most probably always will be. But that can lead to a lot of painful misunderstandings. At times, it can be a real cross.

The Pilgrim

He just turned seventy-one
and is starting to show his age,
yet he has the sense
that an important change
is coming in his life.

His confreres say
that's nothing new.
They say he thought
he'd die at fifty-four
just like his priestly brother did,
and, ever since,
he's been wandering around,
aimlessly.

I know this may be said in jest
and that only a friend
who knows me well
could ever have put it like that,
but still, it hurts
to hear my life described
in such a heartless way.

How can I ever speak with my brothers now
about the wandering Aramean
and the restless-hearted Augustine?

—Last Night I Died

So, whether my religious community, my family, my friends, or even I myself can understand it or not, I'm probably not going to die with my boots on. I'm probably going to die walking barefoot through yet another confusing adventure that I don't fully understand and can't explain, but that, somehow or other I'm being given the courage to welcome.

3

An Image of Who I Am

Lightening the Load

*The first thing we have to do
is to notice
that we've loaded down this camel
with so much baggage
we'll never get through the desert alive.
Something has to go.*

*Then we can begin to dump
the thousand things
we've brought along
until even the camel has to go
and we're walking barefoot
on the desert sand.*

*There's no telling what will happen then.
But I've heard that someone,
walking in this way,
has seen a burning bush.*

—Last Night I Died

Come to think of it, "walking barefoot" really isn't a bad image for how my life has been unfolding over the past seventy-five years. It isn't that I like walking barefoot all that much. That's just how it turns out, especially during times of transition.

During those times it's as though I grow out of my old shoes. They become too tight for me and more and more uncomfortable. They just don't fit anymore. Eventually, the only option I seem to have is to take them off, leave them behind, and start walking barefoot for a while until I can find a pair of shoes that fits me.

When I put it this way it sounds very simple and straightforward, but it's anything but that as I live through it. I often hate to leave my old shoes behind. Even if they're uncomfortable, I've gotten used to them. I may even be thinking they'll last for a lifetime and hate to admit that they won't. I can hear myself saying, "I can certainly get four or five more good years out of these shoes," or "Maybe if I just had them stretched," or, "Better one pair of old shoes on my feet than a pair of brand new shoes down the road someplace," or with growing fear and trepidation, "What if I can't find another pair of shoes that fits me? I don't want to go around barefoot all my life."

Besides, no matter how much experience I've had in changing shoes—and I've had an awful lot—I'm still a tenderfoot when it comes to going barefoot; not just in the beginning either, but every step of the way. I keep thinking that it will be different this time around and that it won't hurt so much. I guess I'm still thinking of my Boy Scout days. I was a tenderfoot then only until I got my stripes. After that, I was a tenderfoot no longer. I was a seasoned hiker. My feet were so hardened by the journey that they were as good, if not better, than shoes. At least I thought they were. I imagined that it would just be a matter of time before I'd be walking barefoot on burning coals.

That was a great thought, but it never worked out that way for me. I may be an Eagle Scout on the books, but in finding my way through life's transitions I'm *still* a tenderfoot—and a pretty awkward one at that. So far, each of my barefoot pilgrimages has felt like another one of my walks to the beach as a child. That was way before flip-flops came along. Anyway, each afternoon we'd walk barefoot on the red-hot sidewalks of Wildwood, New Jersey. We walked all the way from our little rented bungalow on the Bay to the beach and back again. "Ouch, ouch, ouch, ouch...." The red-hot sand wasn't much better, either. It was like trying to cross the Sahara desert barefoot.

That's pretty much what most of my barefoot transitions have been, too. No matter what I expected, the farther I walked the more sensitive my feet became. And not only my feet but my face, my hands, my whole body, and my heart as well. I often felt like I didn't have any skin on anymore. What's worse, I thought everybody noticed it. I could pick up every little vibe, every little comment, every little glance, every little breeze. It was anything but pleasant. Anything but graceful. Anything but fun. It was like having perfect pitch in a chorus that was merrily singing a quarter tone flat. It grated against my nerves.

It was somewhat like that when I took off my dancing shoes on finishing high school and, at eighteen, walked barefoot to the monastery. It was very much that way when I left my American shoes behind at twenty-two and walked barefoot all the way to Rome and then to Paris for graduate studies. It was that way again when I left my badly worn-out shoes in Europe and, at thirty, returned home to walk barefoot into a college classroom as an enthusiastic but pedagogically ill-prepared professor of philosophy and theology. I could hardly believe it but, fifteen years later, there I was again, walking barefoot for over six years in my journey from the classroom to retreat houses, monasteries and meditation centers all over the country. I was on a long pilgrimage in search of a deeper way of living and a different way of teaching spiritually. "Ouch, ouch, ouch, ouch…" practically all the way. It was a real ordeal.

I thought *those* barefoot journeys were a real ordeal. But when I later felt strongly called to a more solitary way of life, the barefoot journey I had to make to get there was even longer and, in many ways, much more demanding. I had to take off my well-shined priest shoes and walk barefoot for about fifteen years until I finally found the simple sandals that I'm wearing now. And that wasn't all I had to take off, either.

God only knows what comes after these sandals. Maybe flip-flops. Or maybe something beyond anything I've ever seen or can anticipate or imagine. That's probably more like it. That's what seems to be keeping me a tenderfoot all the way.

Of course, when I get sick and tired of walking barefoot through transitions I'm always tempted to try on someone else's shoes for size. It isn't long, though, before I hear my pilgrim feet start complaining:

"Fran, don't even <u>think</u> about putting on those shoes. They're not yours. They don't fit you. You're not Thomas Merton, you know. You're also not Paul of Tarsus, or Johann Sebastian Bach, or Mahatma Gandhi, or Jesus Christ, or Thérèse of Lisieux, or Abbot Marmion, or Norbert of Xanten, or Jeremiah, or Martin Buber, or Claude Debussy, or Paul Tillich, or Abraham Heschel, or Augustine of Hippo, or Marc Chagall, or Thomas Aquinas, or Henri Bergson, or Michelangelo, or Georges Rouault, or El Greco, or Bernard Lonergan, or Teresa of Avila, or Guy de Broglie, or Maurice Blondel, or Paul Claudel, or the Baal Shem Tov, or C.G. Jung, or Ira Progoff, or Rainer Maria Rilke, or John of the Cross, or Bruno Barnhart, or Thich Nhat Hanh, or Karl Rahner, or Hafiz, or Ken Wilber, or David Tracy....

...or any of the host of spiritual companions I've loved, admired, walked with, and whose shoes I thought about putting on.

Of course my tender feet were right. No matter what I think, it always turns out to be much better for me to walk barefoot than to limp through life pretending that someone else's shoes fit me "just fine."

I may be walking barefoot through all of these transitions but I'm certainly not "tiptoeing through the tulips," as a movie once pictured Saint Francis of Assisi doing. In fact, whether they fit me or not, I always take my old hiking boots along. I don't like to admit it but they're really more like combat boots than hiking boots. When I've had enough of walking barefoot and my tender feet are killing me, I put on my boots, lace them up tight, and join the crowd by stomping around in self-righteous, self-justifying, and self-aggrandizing protest.

> *Generations have trod, have trod, have trod:*
> *And all is seared with trade, bleared, smeared with toil:*
> *And wears man's smudge and shares man's smell; the soil*
> *Is bare now, nor can foot feel, being shod.*
>   —Gerard Manley Hopkins, *God's Grandeur*

More than anything else that happens along the way, I deeply regret these arrogant, frustrated, angry parades of mine and how much they can hurt the people who are closest to me and anyone else who gets in my way. These tantrums of mine are violent, and tiresome. Even though, deep down, I know they get me nowhere, from time to time, I still lace up my boots and start stomping around.

Thank God, I eventually recognize what I'm doing. Then I sit down, repentantly take off my combat boots, sling them over my shoulder again and, thoroughly chastened for the time being, continue my barefoot journey.

These journeys are hard enough in themselves but, through a bad habit I've developed over the years without even realizing it, I make them even harder. When I find a pair of shoes that really fits me and spend some time breaking them in, I begin to assume that they'll last me for a lifetime. I start thinking that I've finally found the pair of shoes that were made for me and can walk farther than my feet can.

I now realize this is an illusion. No matter what I think about the shoes I'm currently wearing, I always wear them out and have to go barefoot again. But that doesn't seem to keep me from thinking that I've finally found the shoes that will never wear out. So, again and again, I'm surprised when the shoes I've been wearing so comfortably for years don't seem to fit anymore. The journey is hard enough by itself without my weighing it down with wishful thinking like this.

It's too early for me to tell whether it will actually help me or not but I'm now beginning to think that maybe it's not my feet that can walk farther than any pair of shoes I've ever tried on. Maybe it's my restless heart.

I could have saved myself some recurring disenchantment long ago, however, if I had recalled a few of the little proverbs my Dad used to slip me from time to time, especially as he got older. Two that come to mind right away are "This, too, shall pass away, son" and "We have not here a lasting dwelling place."

But, as often happens with proverbs, these two came before I was ready for them. They struck me as "old fashioned." I would have a lot more living to do before I could appreciate their wisdom. Besides, at the time when they could have saved me some grief, I was much too busy building castles in the sand to pay any attention to them.

One proverb that did stick with me all the way, however, and still does, is one that my father embodied for me as long as he lived. "To your own self be true."

It isn't much consolation to me now but, looking back, I can recognize a basic rhythm in the way my life has been unfolding. The academic degree cycle may well have set this rhythm for me early on. I don't know. Anyway, it seems to me that, basically, my life often grows by moving through a four-year cycle. After finding a new pair of shoes that seem to fit, I take a year getting used to them. Then I spend two years or so walking around in them, making a creative contribution in my new setting. Finally, I spend about a year wrapping things up, handing them on, taking off my shoes, and heading out, walking barefoot once again.

Of course, as with all growth cycles, this four-year cycle isn't an ironclad rule but it does seem to be a recurrent rhythm in my life. It's as though my life moves and grows through its own seasons, in its own way, and in its own timing. Realizing that doesn't keep me from having to make the journey but it does help me have a sense of what season I seem to be moving through.

After growing through more of these seasons that I can remember, I find that I'm getting pretty graceful in moving through the Spring times of "hopeful beginnings" and the Summer times of "creative contributions." Where I can see that I still need a lot more work is moving through the Fall and Winter times of "painful endings" so that, whether they're painful or not, they may be times of "graceful endings."

This is the time when I'm most inclined to put on my old combat boots again. Recognizing this, I try to be especially careful and considerate now as I move through these "wrap things up" seasons. It's as though I'm trying to tiptoe so carefully through these very delicate periods that no one will see my footprints.

Being Still

I'm tiptoeing around the hermitage these days,
and around my thoughts and feelings.
Not saying a word.
Moving very carefully.
Like a deer in the forest.
Not making a sound.
Not leaving a footprint.
Not wanting to disturb a soul.
Especially my own.
  —Last Night I Died

Without really knowing it, I was about to enter another one of my "tiptoeing through disenchantment" seasons when I was attending a week-long Intensive Journal retreat led by my friend, Ira Progoff. It was being held at a beautiful retreat center in the heart of the Pocono Mountains in Pennsylvania. The fall was just beginning. The weather, the trees, and the views of the foothills off in the distance were glorious. So was the silence that seemed to engulf me on arriving.

I also had the good fortune of being able to stay in a hermitage which was set off by itself and partially buried in the edge of a cliff that overlooked the valleys below. It was small, clean, and simple. It seemed to be waiting to welcome me. This was an ideal setting for doing the deep inner work that I felt I was being called to do and which I knew Ira's direction would greatly facilitate.

For the first six days Ira led us for six or seven hours a day in progressively deepening cycles of meditation into the heart of own personal and transpersonal experience. Again and again we moved through the clearing muddy water on the surface of our lives into the many-layered well of our inner experience and then back out again. Little by little this inward-outward, downward-upward journey strengthened and enlarged the muscles of my spirit so that they became loose and limber, making me free to move in the inward parts of myself and able to hold and carry whatever I experienced there. Eventually, this meditative journey let me enter the underground stream, a place of more-than-personal communing with my whole life, with all of life, and with the Wisdom of Life itself.

As we gathered for the meditative session on the evening of the sixth day, I felt an atmosphere of great anticipation in the air. It was as though, after doing the meditative work of the previous days, we were ready now for the deepening work we were about to do. I may have been more ready for it than most. Ever since I had met Ira seven years before, I had completely dedicated myself to studying, practicing, internalizing, and teaching this meditative way of growing personally, spiritually, and creatively.

We began the session with an extended conversation that allowed us to review and to correlate much of what we had learned from our work so far. Then Ira introduced the next meditative exercise that we were going to do. The gist of what he said was that just an oak tree grows from an acorn that is hidden deep within the ground, so persons seem to grow from a unique symbol-seed that is hidden deep within each of us.

However, he added, that's not the first place we usually look to try to discover what kind of person we are. The first place we usually look is outside of ourselves as we try to find our place in the world outside and to build a meaningful life there. Without even being aware of it, we naturally do this by imitating others whom we admire for having "made it" in the world. In this way, for better or worse, we build our outside, or conventional, identity. My personal journey had documented that very well,

> *Fran, don't even <u>think</u> about putting on those shoes. They're not yours. They don't fit you. You're not Thomas Merton, you know....*

Ira went on to say that, while we're looking around outside, all the while there is a unique, highly individualized symbol-seed trying to push its was up through the surface of our lives to let us know what kind of person we truly are. We can see how this happens by giving studied attention to how the lives of creative persons actually unfold. These creative lives are very different in all sorts of ways but they all have one thing in common. They all unfold from the inside out. As they do, the lives that creative persons are living let us see how the symbol-seed of their own identity that is buried deep within them is creatively manifesting itself in the world.

Ira then drew several examples of this process from his ten-year study at Drew University of creative persons' lives. He pointed out from the way C. G. Jung's life actually unfolded how he could be seen to be living the inner symbol-seed and myth of the *wise old man*. In a similar way, Martin Buber and Paul Tillich were living the symbol-seed of the *prophet* or the one whose life, work, and awareness is centered on how God relates to the world. Abraham Lincoln and John F. Kennedy, on the other hand, were both living out the symbol-seed of the *hero* and working through the challenges that come with creatively living that myth, often including that of an early death. Dag Hammarskjöld was living out the symbol-seed and myth of the biblical image of the *suffering servant* who gives his life for others. When his spiritual journal revealed this after his tragic death, people who thought of him only as a diplomat and a politician were amazed and edified at the depth from which he actually was living and working. Whenever anyone is deeply living from their own inner image of identity as these persons did, their whole life becomes a creative, symbolic act and event in the world.

Ira then raised the question, "When you look at the inner and outer facts of how your own life is unfolding as we have been doing in this retreat so far, what is the image of identity that is animating your own life?" He pointed out how this kind of question cannot adequately be answered by intellectually analyzing our lives. That would be as fruitless as pulling a plant out of the ground again and again to make sure that its roots were growing correctly. We'd kill it in the process. This kind of question is answered by meditatively going to the underground level where the symbol seed is germinating within us and seeing whether it will answer our question in its own way. When it does, as empiricists of inner experience, we honor it by attentively describing it in our journal just as it is. If it doesn't manifest itself, we honor whatever we experience in that meditative place by recording it in our journal just as it comes to us. With that, we were ready to begin the meditation:

> *The pathway inward is very familiar to me now and I am comfortable following it. It leads me gently into my heart where I am very still and at peace. There is complete darkness and complete silence here. I cannot hear a heartbeat or see or hear anything else. All is still. I am sitting in the silent darkness within my heart, hearing nothing, seeing nothing. But I am not afraid. I sit all alone, waiting in silent attentiveness for I don't know what here in the place of my heart.*
>
> *Now I become aware of another presence here in the darkness. I am no longer alone. Something or someone is in this darkness with me. I don't see it. I don't hear it. I just know it is present here. I know it directly, in a heartfelt way. We are present here together now, sharing the silent darkness....sharing the silent darkness.*
>
> *Then, all of a sudden, a realization breaks through to me with tremendous force. I don't see it. I don't hear it. But I feel it with all my heart. I am a misfit! I am a misfit!*
>
> *This image floods me with delight. I feel as though, all at once, my heart is filled with a blinding light that lets me see even though I don't see anything. It's like being hit by a lightning bolt of animating energy. It's like discovering a great treasure hidden in the field of my heart. It's like nothing I can ever describe.*
>
> *I can hardly contain my joy but, somehow or other, I sit with it, silently describing and savoring what I am experiencing here in the silent darkness of my heart. Then I slowly return once again from this inner darkness to the surface of my life and to the light of the conference room outside.*

When Ira asks if anyone would like to read from what they've written during the meditation, I hesitate. I'm not sure whether or not it wants to be read aloud.

After listening to a few other retreatants read however, I feel strongly moved to read as well.

Reading aloud is still another meditative experience for me. It makes my experience of being a misfit feel even more tangible, more real, and more powerful. It intensifies my experience by letting my body reflect and validate it in its own unique way. It stirs up additional feelings and realizations within me which I take time to note.

As I'm preparing to leave the conference room and return to the hermitage, a distinguished looking middle-aged man comes over to me.

"I was so pleased to hear that you're a mystic," he confides, and adds with a clear sense of satisfaction. "You know, I'm a mystic, too."

"I didn't say 'mystic,'" I reply, "I said 'misfit.'"

"Misfit?" he grimaces, "Oh, my god!" He turns quickly on his heel, and disappears without saying another word. He doesn't have to.

This was my very first hint that others may not share my enthusiasm in realizing that I'm a misfit. To tell the truth, until I did this meditation, I never felt that good about that notion either. There's a definite down side to being a misfit. By that time I knew it only too well from personal experience. That's something that I probably won't have to explain to anyone else.

"Misfit? Oh, my god!"

That makes me realize that there's a very big difference between how "misfit" sounds on the street and how it feels in my heart. On the street it sounds like a crying shame.

"Have you heard about Fran?"
"No. I haven't."
"He's a misfit, you know."
"What a shame. And he used to be such a regular guy."

In my heart, though, it feels like a mysterious seed-symbol that carries the inner coding of how my life is unfolding. It's like having a heartfelt sense of what kind of a person I've been all along and will continue to be, even though I have no idea what outward form that will take from season to season. It's as though my life and I are having a heart-to-heart talk.

> "Fran, do you know who you *really* are?"
> "No. Not really."
> "You're a misfit. That's who you are."
> "A misfit? Whoopee!"

Anyway, on my way to bed that night I make a mental note that it might be better for me not to tell others that I'm a misfit or to try to explain to them the joy and energy it gives me to realize that. That way I would be honoring the wisdom of the Rabbis when they say, "When you discover a new way of serving the Lord, keep it under your heart for nine months." My hunch, though, is that my misfit pregnancy will be much longer than that.

I'm so energized by the evening's meditation that I think I'll have a hard time falling asleep. However, I fall asleep right away, smiling and praising my God,

> *"...I sleep, but my soul watches."*

The next morning I join Ira for breakfast. I reenact for him my meeting with the retreatant the night before. We both have a good laugh over it. "Mystic. Misfit." Ira says. "It's the same. One of them leads to the other."

We both have a good laugh over that, too. But part of me isn't laughing. It knows right away that there's a good deal of truth in what Ira says. If being a "mystic" means being someone who is living a Mystery and knows it, then at least in my case, "misfit" and "mystic" certainly lead to one another.

4

A Most Untimely Birth

Jesus, Mary, and Joseph.

—A Christian Mantra

Seventy-five years ago I was welcomed into this world breathlessly riding on a mantra. As the good Irish woman that she was, my mother seldom spoke about making love, being pregnant, giving birth, or anything "of that sort." But maybe in a weak, loving moment, she made an exception in my case, as she sometimes did.

Anyhow, she confided to me that when I was delivered I was what she called a "blue baby." I think that means that my heart was missing a beat; that I was having a hard time catching my breath in this world; and that I was more or less breathlessly blue all over. I don't get blue anymore, at least not physically, but from time to time, I still have some trouble catching my breath in this strange environment.

So, as I guess was prescribed at the time, the doctor was holding me upside down, anxiously smacking me on the back to get things going. All the while my mother was lying in bed praying, "Jesus, Mary, and Joseph. Jesus, Mary, and Joseph." She always prayed that prayer when the going got tough, and, in her long life of dedication, the going got tough very often. The doctor turned to her and said, "Lady, you'd better start praying for this little guy if you want him to make it."

I guess he didn't think "Jesus, Mary, and Joseph" was a prayer. But my mother did, so my mother just went right on praying "Jesus, Mary, and Joseph" and I was welcomed into this world breathlessly riding on my mother's favorite mantra.

I don't know how my mother's other twelve deliveries went but I do know that mine wasn't, by far, the most dramatic. She delivered one of us—it may have been John—while the hospital was going up in flames and my fireman father was on the floor below fighting to put it out. He didn't find out that Mom was upstairs having the baby until he went home. That's what I call drama. It even made the Philadelphia newspapers. My father must have told me that, even though he didn't speak much either about being pregnant, having sex, giving birth, or anything else "along that line." And he wasn't even Irish. He was German.

My sister Catherine was much more comfortable than Mom was in talking with me about giving birth and "that sort of thing." She told me how she gave birth to one of her older children while calmly eating a sandwich in the back seat of the family car as her husband Jim frantically tried to deliver the baby. It was the first and last time he had to do that. The doctor was good enough to take care of the other six deliveries.

My mother told me that when I came into the world she had trouble right from the beginning with my sense of timing. As an Irish woman she experienced my arrival as a most untimely birth. She had been praying that I would be born on July 11. If God happened to think that was too early, she was willing to hold out until July 13. But, for God's sake, not on July 12. Not on Orangemen's Day! But, as Orangemen's Day dawned, there I came, her little boy blue. Very poor timing.

Later, my mother confessed to me that on the day I was born, she thought to herself, "A fine thing, that! Born on the 12th! This one will never be a good Catholic."

Maybe she was right. Maybe that's why in my old age I'm feeling such a deep passion for experiencing the Unity and Peace that transcends and unites all religions, races, and Peoples.

I know for sure that the first mantra I ever prayed was Mom's "Holy Family" mantra. I didn't start praying it in the delivery room but it couldn't have been much later than that. In fact, my brother Bobby, who arrived twelve months later and much more gracefully than I did, used to join me in praying it out loud whenever we'd hear the fire engines go by. That's what my mother used to do, so I guess we figured we might as well join her.

That's the kind of teacher my mother was, too. She'd just do it and we two little ones would imitate her like chicks following a mother hen. What she taught in that way tended to stick with me, too. I still pray, "Jesus, Mary, and Joseph," whenever I hear the fire engines go by.

"Jesus, Mary, and Joseph," wasn't the only one-liner my mother introduced to us. Whenever she'd say something she hoped to do in the future she'd always add, "If God spares me breath." I really could have used that one in the delivery room. Come to think of it, it would have come in handy, too, in the intensive care unit.

Another one of my mother's one-liners is one of my earliest childhood memories. As she gave Bobby and me our Saturday night bath together in the tub she'd say, "I want you to remember one thing. Marry your own kind."

"Marry your own kind?" At three or four years old, I didn't have any idea what that could mean. By the way my mother said it, though, I knew it was very important so I'd better keep it in mind. Later, I learned that it meant, "Don't marry an Italian girl. We'll have only Irish Catholic girls around here."

So I found it rather funny when, much later, one of my cousins married a handsome young Italian man whom Mom grew to love very much. She could never fit that experience in her "marry your own kind" head, though. She had no trouble at all, however, fitting it in her loving Irish heart. So, whenever she'd pay him a compliment—which was very often—she'd say something like, "Vince is an Italian, *but* he's a great guy," or "...*but* he really takes good care of Theresa," or "...*but* he's a wonderful father."

During the Second World War, another one of my mother's prayerful one-liners was, "Thank God for the warm bed, and the roof over your head."

A Mother's Prayer

"Now thank God for the warm bed
and the roof over your head,"
my mother would say
as she tucked us in,
"Your brother is lying out there
in the trenches."

> We didn't know what "trenches" meant
> but we had no love for that strange word,
> for, as it fell from my mother's lips
> tears fell from her eyes.
>
> So we thanked God for the warm bed
> and the roof over our head.
>   —Last Night I Died

When, as a teenager, I began to realize that I was the center of the whole universe and to act accordingly, Mom would punctuate my bragging, and many of my requests for the money to go somewhere, with another one-liner: "Self, self, self." If I had been more sensitive this could have taken the wind out of my sails, but I seemed to be sailing with a very strong current of hot air at the time. No wise sayings seemed to faze me.

When I got a little older, though, I began to realize that "self, self, self" wasn't just for teenage years. It began having a haunting, perennial quality about it. It embodied a wisdom that challenged me in every season of my life. It was as though "self, self, self" was always crying out within me for "Self, Self, Self," and for the radical re-orienting of my life which that shift in perspective from "Me" to "Thee" inevitably entails.

Maybe in another one of her loving moments—which multiplied as I got a little older—my mother made another exception to her rule of not talking about giving birth and "that sort of thing." Anyway, she told me that, after the poor health that followed her giving birth to Charlie, her doctor told her that having eleven children was enough. He strongly advised her for her own health's sake not to have any more children. So she gave birth to me and then to Bobby right in a row just before her body decided to follow the doctor's orders.

One of my ways of showing my deep love for Mom when I was young was to pitch in and help her, and to thank her for all she was doing for us. One of the things I kept thanking her for, especially when things were going well for me, was for not obeying the doctor's orders and for having the courage to give birth to her twelfth-born, namely me. I wouldn't know what I would have done otherwise.

I never made this connection before but maybe blue became my favorite color right from the day I was born. But when Saint Paul describes himself "as one born out of time," I know first-hand what he's talking about.

One thing I also know is that I owe my life, my breath, and my faith in Christ and God to the beauty and the example of one very loving and heroic Irish Catholic woman. She is the mother not only of my body. She is the mother of my soul. She was my first spiritual director. She taught me not only how to walk, but also how to pray, and how to live. She also taught me to love the ocean even before I could swim.

So, with her very much in mind, when the time comes, I intend to enter the New Life riding on her favorite mantra, "Jesus, Mary and Joseph." And, if God gives me breath, this time I intend to arrive right on time.

5

Two Perennial Questions

"Who made you?" "Why...?"
—*The Baltimore Catechism*

When I was a very little boy I knew a surefire way to earn a nickel. Every time we had guests when my Dad was home, I'd find my way to the parlor. If I lingered there long enough, my Dad was sure to try to edify the guests by inviting me to come over to him. Then I'd stand there at attention and he'd asked me, "Francis, who made you?"

"*God* made me," I'd answer, without batting an eye.

"And tell me, Francis, Why did God make you?" my father would add.

"God made me to know him, to love him, and to serve him in this world, and to be happy with him forever in heaven."

Then the guests would applaud, my father would smile, I'd stick out my little hand, and my father would put a brand new shiny nickel in it. You could buy a lot of candy with a nickel in those days.

If I had been perfectly honest, I guess I would have had to answer the second question somewhat differently. I'd have said, "God made me to know him, to love him, to serve him in this world, and to be happy with him forever in heaven, and to get a nickel for being able to remember all of that."

After a couple of years of school, I found out that that's the way it is with first catechism lessons. I learned that studying catechism is all about repeating what others told me about the life of faith. Basically, I was to memorize word for word "how we do it around here," and in no uncertain terms. It was either verbatim or it wasn't anything.

Much later I learned that, in the ancient Church, there was also a much different, more advanced kind of catechism lesson. It involved personally experiencing the Mystery we were living. These advanced lessons were for adults only; and for adults with hash marks on their hearts, and perhaps even on their hides, for living faithfully. Over the centuries, however, this advanced kind of catechism of the Mystery seems to have gotten lost somewhere.

For instance, it's taken me almost a lifetime to discover that believing isn't a mercenary action. I was made, not only "to know God, to love God, and to serve God in this world," but to do so without any expectation of a handout—without any hope of a payoff. I was made to love God and others in the very same way that God loves everyone, including me—unconditionally, with no strings attached. The fact is that I can't do that on my own. I know because, as hard as I've tried, I've never succeeded in doing it on my own. So, when I find myself loving unconditionally, it must be the Mystery loving through me. In this case, no matter how we may "do it around here," believing isn't "something *we* do around here." It's "something *God* does within us around here."

Basically, the advanced catechism lessons are all about learning how to let this happen. As an adult, I've found loving God and others unconditionally to be one of the secret catechism's hardest lessons to learn. It flies right in the face of all of my instinctive "enlightened self interest" and "I did it my way" ways of relating. I still don't quite get it. But I have no doubt at all that this is really how it's "done unto me and us by God" around here. When I'm not only able to recite this "no strings attached" adult catechism lesson, but actually to experience it, I have to ask, "Now, who did that? It couldn't possibly have been me." And, deep down, I'm right.

But, as old as I am, I still find it very hard to get over my childhood habit of sticking out my hand for a payoff for knowing, loving, and serving God in this world. I find that being a priest hasn't helped that any, either. Whether we're a pastor or not, we priests all seem to have a habit of sticking out our hand. It just comes with the turf.

If, as a much younger person, I thought that I'd eventually grow out of my two childhood catechism questions, as many Catholics do, I was dead wrong. I avoid them from time to time. I even forget them from time to time. But I don't grow out of these two questions. For me, these questions are ultimately unavoidable. They aren't annuals in my life. They're perennials. They keep coming up for me in every time and season. Even if I haven't followed them, these two questions have followed me through my life every step of the way. They've been like the pedal points of my life and the underlying directional signals in all of the transitions I've lived through. "Who made you?" "Why did God make you?" At times, they can be so disturbing. At times, they can be very consoling. But whether they're disturbing or consoling, they just won't go away.

I'm not saying that I've always given a correct or an unqualified answer to these two questions, especially in the way I act. In my many "self made man" seasons, I answer, "God made me" with my lips, while my whole life is singing, "I did it my way." In my innumerable "how great I am" seasons, I answer "to know God, to love God, and to serve God in this world," while at the same time my whole life is shouting, "I'm busy now. I'll get back to you on that later. Don't call me. I'll call you." And in between, I still instinctively stick out my hand. No matter how I answer them, though, these two catechism questions just won't go away.

As they've kept coming back at important times in my life, these two simple questions have become more and more charged for me. They were there when I decided to become a Norbertine. They were there when I changed my major from chemistry to philosophy. They were there when I took my solemn vows. They were there when I was ordained a priest. All the while, I continued to explore them personally in studying and teaching philosophy and theology and in my liturgical and meditative prayer. They emerged again in the doctoral dissertation that I wrote on *Faith and Eternal Life: The Unity of Theological Experience in the Synthesis of Thomas Aquinas*. There, my highly technical answer to these two simple catechism questions was, "God made me to be beatifically transformed by being united with God as my Ultimate Destiny *here and now* through the animating gift of a faith that fills me with God's own hope and love."

If, as a little tyke, I had said that mouthful to my father when he asked who made me, he probably would have been very disappointed.

He would have looked at me bewildered and said, "What?" Not only would he not have rewarded me with a doctorate in philosophical theology but, for the first time ever, he would have let me go up to my room nickel-less.

Come to think of it, even though my professors seemed to appreciate my dissertation, they didn't give me a nickel for it, either. But, nickel or no nickel, it was worth it. It allowed me to learn in considerable detail how Augustine and Aquinas, two of the greatest minds the Christian tradition has ever known, answered these two questions as adults. It also laid a firm foundation for all of my subsequent insights into these two perennial questions.

These days, I'm more and more convinced that God made me so that God could be one with me and I could be totally one with God *here and now*. That's what I hear those who have taken the Gospel to heart and given their lives for it clearly telling me. It's also what I think the secret catechism lessons are basically all about and what the saints and mystics are passionately searching for. It's clearly not one of the things that we can do around here. It's what only God can do around here in ways that we can't even imagine.

For the most part, though, I keep this experience of being one with God under my heart, since, even though it's at the heart of the life of Jesus and the Gospel, it seems to upset those who aren't yet ready to hear it, and it creates a lot of misunderstanding. But, indirectly, I keep trying to point to it since it is such great Good News and such a great relief from a belabored Christianity of personal achievement. Thank God, whether I get a nickel for this or not doesn't matter to me one bit.

The older I get the more forgetful I get but I will never forget these two questions. They're written on my heart.

"Who made you?" "Why did God make you?"

Unforgettable.

6

Leaving the World

*They do not belong to the world
any more than I belong to the world.*

—John 17: 16

At one point in our lives, my sister Catherine and I were like two ships passing in the night. I was just coming into the world and she was about to be invited to leave it.

One of the nuns who taught Catherine in high school asked her to stay after class. "Catherine," the Sister said, "you're a fine young woman. Have you ever thought of becoming a nun?"

"Oh, I really couldn't do that, Sister." Catherine replied. "I love the world too much."

The Sister looked terrified, as if she'd just seen the devil. She put her hand over Catherine's mouth and shouted, "*Never* say that, do you hear? *Never* say that."

So Cass stayed in the world and, as a fine Christian woman, mothered seven beautiful children.

I think it would have been nice if the nun had asked Cass what she meant by "the world," but I guess she was much too shocked at the time to do that. Besides, it was assumed that every good Catholic knew what "the world" meant, and it definitely wasn't something to be loved, especially "too much." Without saying it, what the nun was actually inviting Catherine to do at the time was to "leave the world."

When I got to be Catherine's age, I was accumulating a lot of good reasons for joining the Norbertine community, but "leaving the world" was definitely not one of them. As a child, my very first experience of leaving the world was most unpleasant.

When the Second World War broke out, my brother Tom lied about his age and left high school in his junior year so that he could join the Marine Corps. After finishing boot camp at Parris Island, he came home in his brand new uniform to be with us for a week before being sent to fight in the Pacific. So my father, mother, and Tom piled my younger brother Bobby and me into the car so that Tom could pay a parting visit to my sister Marge. Marge had left high school early, too, to enter the convent.

We drove into the convent grounds in a gentle snowfall and parked at the far end of the parking lot. As we waited there, Dad tried to explain to Bobby and me that only Tom would be allowed to see Margaret. We children were to stay in the car with Mom and Dad and not try to see or talk to her. Otherwise, we would get her in a lot of trouble. She could even get thrown out of the convent.

This made no sense to me at all. It made even less sense to me when I saw Margaret in her white veil slowly walking down the hill at the far edge of the parking lot and Tom in his uniform walking silently through the snow to meet her. They stood there in the falling snow like two statues off in the distance, a young Marine and a young nun. As we sat there looking at them, it got awfully quiet in the car.

After a few minutes Marge turned around and walked back up the hill. Then Tom slowly came back to the car and we drove away. We hardly said a thing all the way home.

As a child, I could make no sense at all of what had just happened, but that picture of the young Marine and the young nun standing alone in the snow is still deeply engraved on my mind.

Much later, I realized that the reason behind this sorry scene was that Marge had "left the world," at least for a while. But even as a child I realized that I wanted no part of that if it had anything to do with what went on in that parking lot and how sad it made my parents and me.

I know for sure that I didn't join the Norbertine community to "leave the world." That never entered my mind. I loved the world. I wasn't able to put it into words at the time but I joined the Norbertines to live and work at the heart of the world. That's what I saw my Norbertine high school teachers doing, and that's what I was strongly drawn to be a part of. Even though many outsiders thought of South Philadelphia as a ghetto, I didn't see the Norbertines standing apart from our neighborhood. I saw them being a big part of it all. The quality of their presence among us gave me heart.

Another thing that I know led me to join the Norbertine community was that I saw their life to be of a piece. It reminded me of the robe of Christ, woven from top to bottom without a seam. As I explored many other options for "what I would become when I grew up," I saw that, in most of them, work was one thing, prayer was another, and life was another. I slowly began to see that, for me personally, there would be a lot of seams in many of the other options I was considering.

So I kept my eye on the Norbertines. I got to know them better from the frequent visits of my brother Joe and some of his fellow Norbertines for coffee after Sunday Masses in the parishes. I also got to know them from serving weekday Masses for them at six in the morning, being in class with them all week long, and working off detention demerits at the Priory more Saturday afternoons than I care to remember. I began to see how working, praying, and living together all seemed to be woven into one piece with them. As a teenager, that was a unity I greatly admired. It was the kind of unity that I deeply desired to have in my own life. I still do.

My vocation to religious life didn't come just from the door that I felt was opening in front of me, however. The doors that were closing behind me were very helpful as well. This has been true of all of the transitions I have worked through since. As I made my way through adolescence, it was as though I was being followed around by a haunting question: "What am I doing here?" It would pop up all the time. It popped up right in the middle of my junior prom, when my friends and I were having "the time of our lives." It popped up in the locker room when some of my buddies were bragging about their sexual exploits. It popped up in the many part-time jobs I had after school and in my conversations with co-workers about what they thought life was all about. It popped up while I was sitting on the steps or on the couch with one of my girlfriends. It popped up when I would visit friends and have a hard time imagining myself living the married life they were clearly enjoying. It popped up when our gang would be walking back in triumph from one of our many post-football-game fistfights. It popped up when I began to experience how much pretending and game playing was involved in dating and how inauthentic and tiresome it could feel to me. It popped up with growing frequency as my senior year in high school started coming to an end.

As these and many other doors kept gently closing behind me, they strongly reinforced the sense I had of the direction in which I was being called to go and the particular form that my own life wanted to take. It was as though the dancing shoes that I had grown to love during my high school years were getting too tight. It was time for me to take them off and to see how it would feel to begin walking barefoot for a while.

As I look at it now, "What am I doing here?" was one of the first of many variations I was to experience on my perennial question, "Why did God make *me*?" Even though it seemed to be negative at the time, actually, the way my "What am I doing here?" question had of closing doors for me was very helpful. It was as though it was saying, "Francis, God didn't make *you* to know him, to love him, and to serve him in this world, *in this particular way*. So just keep moving."

Although I didn't put it this way at the time, it was during these often-tumultuous adolescent years that I think I first experienced being a misfit in "the world" that I had come to know and love. In a sense, I guess I *was* "leaving the world." In one form or another, that's what I would be doing every time I had to go barefoot again. I was "leaving the world" that had been very meaningful to me *for a time*. It seems to me that, right from the beginning, being a misfit-in-motion has always been a very important part of being a misfit for me. Restless heart. Misfit. It's been the same for me. One of them leads to the other.

I didn't have to wait until the end of my senior year in high school, however, to know how I was being called. I knew right from the beginning of my sophomore year. I was sitting around a campfire at a Boy Scout retreat listening to the conference and watching a full moon rise on a beautiful fall night. With a moonlit clarity I couldn't explain, I knew right there and then that I was being called to join the Norbertine community. I also knew that I was going to keep it secret for three years, so that it wouldn't cramp my social life. In those days, if anyone knew that you were going to become a priest, you were a marked man. You were like a leper walking the streets crying out, "Squeaky clean. Squeaky clean." Nobody wanted to dance with you. When you entered a room you could almost feel the colorful conversation change to stained-glass and smell the incense that went with it. That's the last thing I wanted to be put through. It would have felt like the kiss of death to my high school years. So I kept my true vocation under my hat, or better yet, hidden deep within my heart.

I found it very interesting to hear how people reacted when, three years later, I finally told them what I intended to do with my life. I wanted to tell my best friend but he beat me to it. He told me. As we were getting ready to go to a dance, he asked me if I was going to become a priest. When I said I was, he said, "I knew it. Every time a girl gets serious, you back off."

In light of my friend's clairvoyance I would have liked to be able to say that there are no secrets among close friends even if they don't talk about them. But when I told another close friend of mine, he got angry at me and didn't talk to me again for a while. I may be wrong, but I think the truth was that he knew that he was being called to be a priest, too. He just found the full scholarship to a prestigious college that he was offered hard to resist.

The contrast between my Mom's reaction and my Dad's was striking, too. When I told him, my Dad looked at me very intently and said, "Son, I take this sort of thing very seriously." As though I didn't. But I must have fooled him. I guess when he saw me dancing five nights a week he figured that I was eventually going to give him a few more grandchildren.

On the other hand, my mother's reaction was a knowing smile and "Francis, I knew it all along."

I knew she was telling the truth, too. It was characteristic of her to keep my secrets until I felt ready to tell her about them. I guess I *can* say that there were no secrets between Mom and me, at least from Mom's side. As she would often tell me, "Francis, I know you like the back of my hand." I think she may have liked me, too.

The most surprising reaction of all came from the parish priest when I asked him to give me a letter of recommendation for the seminary. He looked at me and asked, "Why do you want to become a priest? You're good looking. You could have a woman....you know, everyone will call you 'Father' but you're not really a father until you have a kid....and besides, as a priest, you'll have a lot of superiors bossing you around just like the Bishop bossed me around for as long as he lived...but I got even with him. I stood by his coffin in the middle of the night and told him in no uncertain terms what I really thought of him...."

I have no idea what I made of all of this at sixteen years old. In fact, it was only thirty years later that I remembered it had ever happened. I guess I must have been in shock. All I know is that, in spite of all that Father said, I still wanted to become a priest. Father must have recognized that too, since he gave me a positive recommendation to join the Norbertine community. It must have been meant to be.

I may have had no intention whatsoever of "leaving the world" when I joined the Norbertines but, as seminarians in the 1950s, *not* "leaving the world" took some doing. First of all, Saint Norbert Abbey was strictly cloistered at that time. That meant that no "outsiders" were allowed inside, especially women. The "world" can get awfully small that way.

In addition, we weren't allowed to speak with any of our lay classmates at the College. The fact that some of these lay students were our lab partners or the people we would eventually be ministering to didn't seem to make any difference at all. This was a matter of principle.

After my first two years of novitiate, which was a kind of intensive retreat away from family and friends—or "boot camp" as my brother Tom put it—I was allowed to go back to Philadelphia for a brief vacation. With each visit, I felt that I was getting more and more out of touch with the people and the world I had known. Paradoxically, I was being educated further and further away from the people I thought I would eventually be serving. This was especially true after I had spent eight years overseas studying theology and returned home as a priest. Talk about being out of touch. It took me a while to become fluent in English again. Once I even made the fatal mistake of pronouncing the last name of the Colt's famous quarterback, Johnny Unitas, in Latin. Johnny *Unitas*. That made him sound like an ecumenical movement instead of a football player. After a very awkward pause, that was the end of that conversation. I was beginning to feel like a thoroughly clericalized foreigner in my own neighborhood, a real misfit.

Even though my own mother called me "Father" from the day I was ordained, she had a very straightforward way of putting things in perspective for me. After the guests left the reception after my first Mass, she invited me to join her at the kitchen table for a cup of tea.

"Father Francis," she said, "I want you to remember one thing. You wouldn't have that collar," she said, pointing to my clerical collar, "if I didn't have this ring," she added, showing me her wedding ring.

I've never forgotten that "one thing." This was one of the most graphic and eloquent theology lessons I'd ever had. In it, I heard my mother saying much more than that the sacraments of marriage and ordination are intimately related in Christ. I heard her saying that she was my first priest. And she was. She nurtured me in the faith long before I ever met an ordained priest. Frankly, I think she also was my first bishop. She ordained me in living faithfully long before I even knew what a bishop was.

In reply, I must have said something like, "Okay, Mom," and continued sipping my tea. I may even have bitten my tongue. I know if I had said something like, 'Thanks Mom, that's very profound sacramental theology," she would have replied, "You and your stupid education!" She would say that every time I started using big words. My mother had a very straightforward way of putting things in perspective for me.

Even though I wasn't able to avoid them very well, deep down I was never really converted to the conventional spiritualities of "leaving the world" and of clerical superiority that were so much a part of the popular Catholic culture at that time. The problem was that, in the fifties, they were practically the only show in town. I not only kept bumping into them but just by being a priest I was part of them. But I knew that I couldn't trace that "fleeing the world," or *"fuga mundi"* tradition to Jesus. I couldn't trace it to the one who lived and died so that the world would be one with God, and who prayed to the Father, not to take his disciples *out* of the world, but to consecrate them in the truth. I couldn't trace it back to the God who created the whole world and "saw that it was good." I couldn't trace it back to the Father who so loved the world that he gave his only Son to transform it.

I don't think it can even be traced back to the desert mothers and fathers. It's true that they were deeply disenchanted with the mores of the decadent Roman Empire and with the Christendom that was beginning to imitate it. In that context, these prophets were some of our greatest misfits. It's also true that they felt called to witness heroically to the spiritual truth of the Christian way of life just as the martyrs had done for several centuries during the persecutions. But I think they were led into the desert somewhat as Moses was, not just to flee the world, but primarily to be a liberating light to others and to consecrate themselves to the creative Truth that grounds the world as it shines in the darkness.

I knew I couldn't trace this *"fuga mundi"* spirituality back to Saint Augustine either, even though some keep saying that it all started with him. For him, *The City of God* may have been the tale of two cities but it was the story of one world, the world in which he spent a lifetime whole-heartedly loving, serving, praying, and teaching.

The way I see it, the authentic "leaving the world" tradition is not a lesson in geography at all. It's a lesson in spirituality. To "leave the world" in this sense is to become part of an underground movement at the heart of the world. It's to become part of a quiet revolution dedicated to transforming from the inside out the vision and values that animate this world. For me, to "leave the world" in this sense is to take the low road to becoming a misfit.

But, somewhere along the way, the "leaving the world" tradition started seeing double. It began seeing not one, but two worlds. As a seminarian in the fifties I had been enculturated into that double vision.

The only thing that did for my unarticulated awkward feeling of being a misfit was to make it more pronounced.

Underneath it all, however, I slowly began to realize that my own Gospel vocation is to "be *in* the world, but not *of* it." It was only much later that I realized that this vocation is the deepest source within me of the joyfully liberating sense that I have of being a misfit in the world.

As a seminarian and a young priest I would experience negative feelings of not fitting in from time to time, but I didn't give them very much attention. I didn't have time to do so. I was living a very full, rewarding, and enlightening new life. I was getting to know the ninety or so new Norbertine brothers of my newly-extended family. I also was observing a full schedule of monastic prayer and work, learning to survive the winters in northern Wisconsin, discovering philosophy, completing three college majors in four years, and eventually doing a doctorate in philosophical theology. I didn't have time for much else. At the time, this was the way in which we fleshed out the proverb that our grade school sisters had drilled into us: "An idle mind is the devil's workshop."

My haunting question, "Francis, what are you doing here?" didn't go away in my days as a seminarian and a young priest. Whenever it did pop up, I would go to my room, close the door, kneel by the window, gaze out prayerfully into the night, and ask, "Lord, to whom shall I go?"

From the darkness of the night, the answers that kept coming back were, "Go to no one but me," and "Come to me you who are weary and heavy burdened, and I will give you rest."

So I did just that. Then I went back to doing what I felt God was calling me to do.

So much for "leaving the world."

7

Changing My Name

To the victor I shall give some of the hidden manna;
I shall also give a white amulet upon which is inscribed
a new name which no one knows
except the one who receives it.

—Revelation 3: 17

The biggest change I ever went through in my life took place on the day when I became one with the Risen Christ and he became one with me in Baptism. It really was my wedding day. I would like to have marked it by changing my name, as a lot of blushing brides do, but I didn't have a name to change. It's hard to imagine but it's true. After being welcomed into this world, I went around nameless for two whole weeks. I wasn't socializing much, though, so being nameless didn't make that much difference to me. People seemed to be perfectly content just to make faces at me, call me "baby" and something like "gitchy, gitchy goo" and leave it at that.

So I went around for two whole weeks as "No-name." Of course, I had a last name, but that didn't count. That was my tribal name, and the whole tribe wasn't being baptized; I was. As everybody knows, being baptized into Christ is like taking a bath. It's a deeply personal, one-on-one sort of thing. The priest almost drowns you.

Anyway, being "No-name Dorff" for two weeks made me very curious about what the priest would call me at my christening. So I was greatly relieved when I heard him say, right in the middle of dousing me with living water, "Francis, I baptize you in the name of the Father, and of the Son, and of the Holy Spirit. Amen."

The Abbot of the community of Saint Norbert Abbey evidently thought otherwise.

As I knelt before him seventeen years later asking to be engaged to the Norbertine community for two years, instead of dousing me with water again, he gave me a long white monastic robe that I had to change into right there and then. That made hunting for a new pair of shoes look like child's play. Anyway, when I came back from the sacristy wearing the habit of Prémontré and knelt before the Abbot again he solemnly announced, so that the whole church could hear it, "Francis, from now on, you will be called....Wilfrid."

Maybe it was my imagination but I thought I heard a deep sigh go through the whole church. It was nothing compared to the sigh that went through my heart. "Wilfrid?" I thought. "I'm not Wilfrid, I'm Francis." But what the Abbot declared in those days was said and done, regardless of how beautiful "Francis" began to sound to me.

At that time, that's how it was when you joined the Order. Just like in the Bible, when you made as radical a change of life as this, you got your name changed, whether you liked it or not. That's how it had been in our monastic tradition for over eight hundred years. And that's how it continued to be for me for thirteen long years.

I've never heard any theologian try to make the case that one of the most momentous changes that the Second Vatican Council made in the Roman Catholic Church was to allow monks and nuns to go back to their baptismal names. It sure felt that way to me, though, when I received a surprise letter from the Abbot while I was studying in Paris. In it he told me that he was giving me the option to go back to my baptismal name if I chose to do so since, as important as religious vows are, Baptism is still the change of changes in a Christian's life.

Before you could say "Wilfrid," I fired a letter back to the Abbot gratefully informing him that, from now on, I'd like to be called "Francis" again.

"Francis." What a beautiful name. "François" wasn't all that bad, either. Neither was "Francesco." "Franz" felt a little Prussian to me but it beat "Wilfrid" by a mile. I felt like going out to dinner that night to celebrate the return of "Francis." And I certainly would have, too, except that I didn't have any money.

They say that I was the very first member of the community to return to my baptismal name. No wonder. I'm a "Francis" to the core.

Anybody can see that. I never was a "Wilfrid" to the core, or to anywhere else, for that matter. I don't mean to criticize Saint Wilfrid in any way, though. After all, he *was* a holy English bishop. I don't doubt that "Wilfrid" sounded better with a British accent.

What my family name, my baptismal name, and my religious name all had in common was that somebody else gave them to me. When things really got complicated was when I began choosing a name for myself. I think it all started when, at twelve, I became old enough intentionally to ratify my baptismal vows. I guess I was thought finally to have reached the age of reason. Anyway, as part of my important passage into adulthood as a follower of Christ, I was asked to choose a Christian middle name for myself.

I took this as an important responsibility and gave it a lot of thought. My mother did too. She was very subtly pushing "Matthew," which she kept telling me was "such a beautiful name." I not so subtly declined her invitation, though, just as my eight brothers before me had and my one brother after me would. My reason for doing so was pretty simple. I didn't like the sound of it.

To be honest, at that time liking the sound of it was probably my primary criterion for choosing my middle name, and a lot of other things, for that matter. For no reason at all, a name that kept coming to my mind was "Xavier." That would make me "Francis Xavier." There was great precedent for that combination of names. Saint Francis Xavier, an outstanding early member of the Society of Jesus, seemed to like it very much. He lived his whole life with it.

So, as the Bishop gave me a symbolic slap in the face that confirmed that I was ready and willing to take some heavy hits for Christ, I was officially confirmed "Francis Xavier Dorff."

Even though I chose it myself, it wasn't long before I began having some real problems with this name. First of all, I hadn't realized that this would mean that my middle initial would be "X"—as in "X marks the spot," or "my X wife or husband," or "X this guy out."

It also meant that people would keep asking me what the "X" stood for. That could become quite bothersome, especially if they then wanted to know who "Xavier" was, since I knew very little about him. The Francis I really loved and admired was Francis of Assisi, but it was pretty clear why I didn't want to be known as Francis Assisi Dorff—especially in our neighborhood.

My first solution to this problem was to keep the "X" publicly but secretly to take Francis of Assisi as my patron saint. Nobody else had to know about it.

What I didn't notice at first was that in all of this name changing there was a much deeper name-changing that was going on within me quite independently. From the very first time I heard about it, I've been deeply fascinated by the biblical way of considering a name to be a sacred symbol of the Mystery of a person. From that perspective, to know someone's name is to have a certain power over them, and to invoke a person's name is to evoke the presence and the power of the Mystery they embody.

This perspective is probably about as far as you can get from the conventional American understanding of a person's name as their social ID. But it let me better appreciate the ancient Hebrew tradition of never mentioning the unpronounceable Sacred Name of God aloud, and of referring to the Holy One only indirectly by using one of a very long list of alternative names. It also let me appreciate more deeply the Roman Catholic tradition of it being a sin to mention the Name of God "in vain." The Mystery can't be named.

This got me wondering about what *my* sacred, or unmentionable, name is. My wondering intensified when I learned that certain ancient cultures not only give a similar symbolic importance to a person's name as the Bible does, but that they also distinguish between the person's public names and their secret name. They let anybody know their public names but they share their secret name only with those with whom they are most intimate. It's as though, on the one hand, they have a public family last name. On the other hand, they have a public personal first name. But their mystical name is in the blank space in-between these two. From the outside, they may appear to be persons without a middle name. But from the inside, they and their intimates know better.

When I began to cultivate this frame of mind, it was as though I began bowing inwardly to every person I met, including myself. It was as though I was a Mystery honoring another Mystery. That's how it was, and that's how it still is.

For a long while, I tried to imagine what my sacred or secret middle name could possibly be. Over the years, many names kept coming to mind and I walked with each of them for a while.

First there was "Emmanuel"—God with us. I love that name. Then there was "Shalom"—the well-being of God's Peace. When I said it, I felt it. Then there was "Nemo"—"nobody" or "the nameless one." My metaphysics professor first called me that when I would forget to write my name on the test paper. As I walked with "Nemo" for a while, I was never really sure whether it wanted to be my secret middle name or my first name, or my only name. It felt that it could also have belonged to someone else who just wanted to walk with me for a while and teach me some hidden things I needed to know.

Much later, when I was studying the desert Mothers and Fathers, "Nemo" showed up again. He must have been ordained a priest in the meantime since he returned as *"Abba* Nemo"—"Father Nobody," an unknown desert Father. He even gave me a whole book of pseudo desert stories for which I was most grateful. They were "pseudo" because I wrote them.

> *A woman once asked Abba Nemo, "Abba Nemo, how am I to love my husband?*
>
> *"You are to love your husband with passionate detachment," Abba Nemo replied.*
>
> *"Passionate detachment?" the woman objected, "That's stupid."*
>
> *"Yes, I know," Abba Nemo said, "but that is how you are to love your husband."*
>
> *"Then I guess I am to love my God with pure detachment," the woman continued.*
>
> *"Oh, no," Abba Nemo replied. "You are to love your God with pure passion. With pure passion."*

I always liked the name "Abba Nemo." I still do. It conjures up for me being no one, living no where, knowing nothing, doing nothing, yet, somehow or other, when he's around, everything gets done. The fact that this name may have been given to me by the desert Mothers and Fathers made it special, too. Much later, Abba Nemo gifted me with an intimate prayer phrase,

There's nothing between us now.
Absolutely nothing.

Later on "Shalom" also paid me another visit. Actually, it was with me all along, but, from time to time, it would come to me with added force, as charged names and words like that often do.

This time, it came back in a different language. I was beginning a sabbatical year in Berkeley, California, during which I hoped to get my health back, to sort out why I was feeling so disenchanted with teaching in an academic setting, and to figure out what I could possibly do about it.

While I was sitting at lunch in the University cafeteria dressed so that no one in the world would ever suspect that I was a priest, a Jesuit priest came over, introduced himself, and asked if I was a priest. So much for my perfect disguise. I invited him to join me for lunch.

He was from Japan and had come to the States to do graduate work in philosophy. We had a wonderfully stimulating conversation. It was as though we had known one another for a long time. In the course of our conversation, we got talking about the symbolic importance that the Japanese culture gives to a person's name. So I asked him, "If someone wanted to be called 'he who loves peace' what would his name be in Japanese."

He looked at me in disbelief. "That's *my* name!" he said. "Kazumi."

We just sat there and looked at one another for a while. Then he said that the way the Japanese say it is "The one born for peace." He wrote his name down for me in both English and Japanese. He also pronounced it for me several times until I finally got it right.

As we parted, I thanked him whole-heartedly for his visit. I felt that he had given me a most mysterious gift from Japan in a most mysterious way at a most appropriate time.

That wasn't the only Japanese name I've been given, either. As I finished a course in Japanese calligraphy fourteen years later, the teacher gave me a beautiful Japanese name, as she did all her students. As the master teacher that she was, she gave me a lot more than that, too.

Seasons come and go
as my teacher glides her brush
over rice paper.
 —Last Night I Died

In my old age, I've now become much more comfortable with the empty space between Francis and Dorff. I no longer need to fill that void with something that sounds good to me or pleases others. It likes to be empty to welcome the treasured names in my growing litany that keep visiting me. It also continually reminds me that while the Mystery that I'm living is many-splendored, it's not a thing. The Mystery has many names, but it's not a name. The Mystery's true reality cannot even be pronounced, much less explained. It dwells in the empty space between all the names I have and all the names I give it. That's just how it is.

There's nothing between us now.
Absolutely nothing.

I can live with that.

8

Being a Stranger in a Strange Land

I am a stranger in the land.

—Psalm 119: 19

Although it's a good way to become one, I wasn't sent to Europe to become a misfit. In many ways I already was one. What I was sent overseas for was to get a doctorate in theology so that I could teach in our seminary and college. The fact that this intensified my experience of being a misfit was an unintended by-product.

I imagine everyone who goes to a foreign land feels like a misfit at first, at least until they get settled and learn the language. I know, deep down, I did, even when I didn't realize it or was doing my best to keep it a secret. Being a misfit was a fact of life. It came with being a stranger in a strange land.

Charlie, a Jesuit priest who was doing the doctorate in Paris with me, gave me a very graphic description of how he experienced this. He said that whenever he'd speak with a French person, they'd hear his accent and ask right away where he was from. When he said, "the United States"—"*clink*"—he'd feel an iron fence go down between them. The same thing would happen when they'd find out that Charlie was a practicing Catholic—"*clink*"—a priest—"*clink*"—and, of all things, a *Jesuit* priest!—"*clink, clink.*"

With five sturdy iron fences between them from then on, Charlie said that there was no hope of their ever being able to relate person-to-person. It was like this for him the whole four years he was in Paris. Part of it probably was due to the fact that he never did learn to speak French very well. But that wasn't the whole story. It seems to me that what he was describing is true of any experience of bias or prejudice of any kind. As soon as you hear "clink," you know that genuine dialogue is no longer possible.

So Charlie started hanging out with Catholic Americans; mostly Jesuits. This didn't help his French at all.

His very gifted brothers at the Jesuit House of Studies had for a long time been observing how confreres came and went. They developed a whole theory of what they might well have called, "The Long-term Cultural Non-adjustment Process" that Americans went through in coming to Paris. I thought it was a remarkably perceptive piece of work.

They maintained that when confreres first arrived in Paris they became "Ugly Americans" for a while. They went around complaining about everything in Paris and saying how inferior or primitive it was compared to what we had in the States. One of the newcomers even complained about how independent the French were. "Look at this," he said with great disdain, "all of these signs in French!"

This first stage could be a very ugly time in the cultural non-adjustment process.

After they'd settled in a bit, however, these "Ugly Americans" began to think they were Frenchmen. In fact, they began to act as though they were more French than the French were. This is pretty hard to do and even harder to take.

In this stage, they let it be known that they were thoroughly embarrassed by American tourists and visitors. They considered them to be most unsophisticated, if not culturally deprived. They did everything they could to avoid these guests and to pretend that they themselves weren't Americans when any other Americans were around.

This second phase was a very awkward and embarrassing time in the cultural non-adjustment process, not for these "Meta-Frenchmen" of course, but for almost everybody else.

When they finally returned to the States, these "Meta-Frenchmen" became discontented strangers in their own homeland. They went around complaining about how the States wasn't at all like Paris. This, of course, was news to nobody else. In fact, most people kept wondering why these Meta-Frenchmen didn't go back to Paris.

As long as it lasted, this third phase was a very annoying time in the cultural non-adjustment process, especially for well-adjusted Americans who had never been to France.

Of course, the process took on a completely different character if, somewhere along the way, one of these misplaced persons came to realize that, actually, he wasn't a Meta-Frenchman. He actually was an American in Paris, or an American who had lived in Paris for a while. Realizing this changed the whole nature of the story.

As I look at it now, this admirable description of the Cultural Non-adjustment Process (C.N.P.) seems to me like a very good recipe for the making of a long-term misfit, at least on a cultural level.

I can honestly say that I don't think I ever was an Ugly American, or a Meta-Frenchman, or even a Meta-Italian, for that matter. My mother would have been pleased to hear that, but I don't claim any credit for it. It's just doesn't seem to be part of my nature.

That doesn't mean that I wasn't a misfit in Europe, though. It just means that being a misfit seemed to be working at a much more basic level in me. It seemed to be working so deeply in me that I often was hardly even aware of it. But aware of it or not, I still was a stranger in a strange land.

What may have helped me a lot in coping with this experience was an insight that I got during my first year in Rome. We were a community of about twenty-five Norbertines from about a third that many countries, living in the Norbertine Generalate on Rome's ancient Little Aventine Hill. During my first year there, I saw that the guys were clearly taking two very different paths in being strangers in a strange land. The majority had quickly cased the situation and had decided that this was going to be a real ordeal that they would just have to endure for a few years and that the best way to survive it was to hang loose and not to commit themselves to anything. They were just misplaced persons "passing through."

As I saw it, this was a very understandable way of psychologically never leaving home. But I was afraid that, for me, it might lay a foundation for a whole life of non-commitment, no matter where I would go.

Perhaps somewhat naively, a few others seemed to decide that, in going through this ordeal, they were going to take the road less traveled and be totally present to the experience as if this was where they would be for the rest of their lives. If they could, they were going to make the best of it and try to get all that they could out of it. I believe that taking this path made the going much tougher.

For whatever reason, I took the road less traveled, and it made all the difference in my life. For better or worse, it rooted me firmly in the present place, time, and circumstances, no matter where I was. It let me learn to live with the perennial questions, "Is this where I really am?" and "Is this how it really is?" as well as with the simple "yes" or "no" answer and the appropriate action that these two questions evoked in me. Taking the road less traveled didn't keep me from living as a stranger in a strange land, however. It actually intensified that experience, but it also made it more creative for me, and that made all the difference.

It may sound rather stupid, but another experience that helped me a lot right from the beginning came from living in Rome for several years in very close quarters with a somewhat older, very angry, and, what I later recognized to be, highly neurotic confrere. As psychologically unsophisticated as I was at twenty-four, this was an awful lot for me to handle.

One of the ways in which my confrere would handle his difficulties was periodically, for what seemed to me to be no reason at all, to give me a cold shoulder that would make the Antarctic seem tropical. It was so cold that I would sometimes have a hard time sleeping, eating, or even studying. Then I would go to his room and ask him whether I had done anything that had offended him and, if I had, tell him that I wanted to apologize for it.

He would inevitably say no, sometimes in a very upset way, but that didn't change his behavior or my dilemma at all. It just made it more disturbing to me.

One morning, when I was feeling especially troubled by this relationship, I visited one of my favorite museums and went directly to my favorite room. It's an extremely beautiful and peaceful room. That morning it was filled with sunlight. I had it all to myself, too, except for the magnificent company of Roman and Etruscan bronze statues that encircled me. They in no way disturbed the very profound silence in the room, though. In fact, their presence greatly enhanced it.

After visiting with each of the statues, I stood for a while gazing quietly into the shallow, mosaic-lined, reflecting pool that was in the center of the room. Then, as if from the silence itself, the words came to me, "I will apologize for anything I do or anything I say that is hurtful. But I will *not* apologize for existing."

At that moment, I felt I became a metaphysician.

This experience opened a path for me through my eight years as a stranger in strange lands. It made me resolve to walk as faithfully as I could to who I really am.

"I will not apologize for being an American in Italy."

"I will not apologize for having to study three hours before and three hours after every lecture my best professor gives in order to have some vague idea of what he's talking about."

"I will not apologize for being a somewhat naïve and idealistic young man who has led a sheltered life up until now and is still wet behind the ears."

"I will not apologize for falling in love with Rome and Paris."

"I will not apologize for believing in Christ or for being a priest of the living God."

"I will not apologize for being my Self."

"I will not apologize for being a stranger in a strange land."

"I will not apologize for being an American."

"I will not apologize for feeling like a misfit."

"I will not apologize for existing."

The litany goes on and on. It's how it really is for me.

This experience in the company of my magnificent bronze friends helped me an awful lot in weathering the many challenges of my years abroad. Together with taking the road less traveled, it made all the difference in my life.

About thirty-five years later, when I was Novice Master in our community in Albuquerque, New Mexico, I used to regale the novices with stories of how it was in "the good old days." They hated them, of course, but I knew that these stories were part of our family history and that it was important to share them with our newcomers.

One story I always liked to tell our novices was about how I was sent overseas for studies. Father Abbot called me in one day and told me that the day after I took Solemn Vows I would go to Rome to get a doctorate in theology.

"You will not come home until you get the degree. Do you understand, Frater?"

"Yes, Father Abbot."

"And if your mother dies, you will not come home. Do you understand, Frater?"

"Yes, Father Abbot."

"And if your father dies, you will not come home. Do you understand, Frater?"

"Yes, Father Abbot."

"And if your priest brother, Father Joseph, dies, you will not come home. Do you understand, Frater?"

"Yes, Father Abbot."

"You will not come home until you get the degree. Do you understand, Frater?

"Yes, Father Abbot."

"Then you may go, Frater."

"Yes, Father Abbot."

"Those were the good old days," I would add, with feigned nostalgia.

Once, after I had told this story, one of my young novices who was from Mexico commented, "And you know what I would have said to him?"

"No," I answered. "What would you have said?"

"I would have said, 'And how 'bout if you die, Father Abbot? Can I come home, then?'"

Times had clearly changed.

As it happened, my father did die while I was in Rome. He died of a heart attack just a few months before I was to be ordained a priest. As the Abbot and I had agreed, I didn't go home.

One of the reasons why I was sent to Rome in the first place was that one of our most brilliant students had just come home from there with a nervous breakdown. I was being sent back to replace him. The fact that, intellectually, I couldn't hold a candle to this guy didn't seem to bother anyone but me. I felt like an amateur wrestler being sent into the ring to replace a real pro toward the end of a fight that he was badly losing. I guess I was hoping that somebody would at least say, "Good luck!"

So before I left, I went to the Dean of the College and asked for his blessing. He was a Norbertine priest and a deeply spiritual man. I knelt down before him in his office and he gave me a most heartening blessing.

When I looked up, I saw a simple crucifix mounted on the wall behind him. Beneath it were the hand-written words of the Psalmist, "*Quem timebo?*" "Of whom shall I be afraid?" I took this phrase to heart. It went with me all the way to Europe. And it still goes with me. Especially when the going gets tough.

Although, in sending me to Europe the Abbot really emphasized the importance of my getting the degree, personally, I never really felt that that was my primary mission. I thought that my mission in going overseas was to grow by learning all that I could. What I didn't realize at first was that it wasn't *what* I learned in Europe that was most important. I've since forgotten most of that.

What was most important for me was becoming aware of *how* I learned whatever I learned. From my second year in Rome on, this emphasis on the way, or process, of how I learned was my primary focus of concern and it has remained that in all that I have learned and taught ever since.

In general, I can say that, during my eight years overseas, it seemed to me that I learned whatever I learned by continually being stretched. Being stretched again and again, often far beyond my physical, emotional, intellectual, personal, cultural, and spiritual limits. I learned by continually being stretched between believing and understanding; between knowing and not knowing; between one culture and another; between praying and living; between fidelity and creativity; between what was and what is; between what is and what might be. Being a stranger in a strange land was a no-nonsense teacher for me.

To say that I found being continually stretched like this stressful would be putting it mildly. As I got off the ship when I finally came home, my mother met me at the dock in New York and greeted me by saying, "Francis, you don't look half as bad as they said you would."

"What?" I thought to myself. "I don't look half as bad as they said I would? I'm twenty-five pounds underweight, pretty much worn out at thirty, and look like I just got released from a concentration camp. How bad did they say I would look?"

I guess the word had gotten out. I had been stretched.

Even though he didn't know it, one of my teachers who was extremely helpful to me in making me conscious of how I learned was Father Bernard Lonergan, a Jesuit professor at the Gregorian University in Rome. He was one of the most brilliant English-speaking theologians of the twentieth century. Although he taught all of the major courses in dogmatic theology, the focus of his own interest and lifework was on the process and method of *how* we come to understand whatever we come to understand and living intelligently and faithfully.

At first, I had the hardest time getting what he was driving at. Talk about being stretched. Besides, at the time, all of our courses and seminars were taught in Latin and, when he taught in Latin, Father Lonergan seemed to me to make no concession at all either to pedagogy *or* to Latin, or to the "obtuseness," as he would say, of his students. I saw right away, however, that he was the theologian's theologian at the Greg. So, even though I needed special permission to do so, I made it a point to take all the courses and graduate seminars that he offered. His profoundly thoughtful presentations laid a firm foundation for my life-long interest in the process and method of *how* we learn whatever we learn.

When my primary focus shifted from *what* I learned to *how* I learned, I found that some of my best teachers weren't professors at all. They were the people, the languages, the culture, the history, the music, the art, the architecture, and the beauty in the cities, towns, and abbeys, in which I lived or which I visited. Among these teachers was also the awesome natural beauty of the Alps, the Pacific Ocean, the Mediterranean Sea, and the Italian, French, Austrian, German, Swiss, English, and Irish countryside. There are no classrooms that can contain the kind of learning these teachers provide.

When I am collaborating these days with artists in trying to bridge the chasm that has opened up between art and Christian religion, they often ask me whether or not I'm an artist myself. I answer, "No. But I've been blessed to have lived for a long time surrounded by great beauty."

As I studied them, many of the churches and sacred sites of Rome taught me more about how the Church grows than any book I've ever read. It was as though some of these ancient churches became channels of living history for me.

On the outside some of the churches were so unremarkably plain that I might easily have thought that they had nothing to teach me. On the inside, however, would be a recently renovated, carefully maintained, sixteenth century church that was alive with worshipping Christians. Underneath this, in the crypt, I could see evidence of the foundation of an earlier Gothic and then Romanesque church on which the present one had been built. Still deeper down into the earth, I could touch some of the stones of the pagan temple that had been razed so that the original Church could be built on this sacred site. Perhaps deeper down still, I would find evidence of a Roman house church, an early Christian cemetery, or a catacomb in which martyrs were buried and early Christians had worshipped.

As I gradually came back up to the surface I would feel that, layer by layer, I was climbing up through time and through the way in which the Church herself grows—embracing and creatively transcending what *was* to build a more contemporary dwelling place for God. This was a powerfully graphic experience for me of how the whole Christian

Community grows by continually being stretched. As I describe it now, I'm there again.

As long as I live, I will never forget the many-layered churches of Rome and the way they showed me how both the Church and I grow by continually being stretched by being strangers in a strange land.

9

Experiencing a Communal Change of Heart

> *The joys and the hopes, the griefs and anxieties of the persons of this age, especially those who are poor or in any way afflicted, these too are the joys and hopes, the griefs and anxieties of the followers of Christ.*
> —The Second Vatican Council

I can't claim any credit for it but when I arrived in Rome in the fall of 1957, the Catholic community was experiencing a major change of heart. This change of heart wasn't all that visible on the surface yet, but it had been going on underground for a century or so, and was now beginning to gain real momentum. It involved turning completely around toward the modern world and other religions and facing them with openness, intelligence, compassion, and respect. This turning around marked a momentous change of direction for a community that had been resolutely "leaving the world" in disenchantment and defensiveness for well over four centuries. It marked a major communal conversion.

For over a century this change of heart had been slowly stretching our Catholic community toward a radical renewal of our spiritual lives by moving us simultaneously in two directions. On the one hand, through the modern scientific methods of historical and literary criticism, we were moving backward through centuries-old layers of bias, misinterpretation, obscurantism, infidelity and legalism to root ourselves anew in the original meaning of the biblical and liturgical sources and the greater-than-personal energy of our Christian tradition. On the other hand, we had begun compassionately reaching outward in faith toward the modern world through a renewed experience of the Mystery of a God who so loved the world that He became one of us to be part of it. As a community of faith, our efforts toward renewal were stretching us in two directions.

As I experienced it, this two-fold movement of "rooting and reaching" was stretching our community toward much more than a simple "updating." It was stretching us toward a radical change of heart. That became quite apparent when the shape that our conversion was to take surfaced and began to manifest itself in the deliberations of the Second Vatican Council.

Over the centuries, the Catholic Church has been called by many names. The most important names for me, however, are not the names others call us. The most important names are the ones we have called ourselves over the centuries to try to express the Mystery of our being. This long litany of names and name changing tells me that, just like with any mystery of an individual, no one name can tell the whole story.

For me, a powerful symbol of our community's contemporary change of heart was that it decided to change its name as well. It was as though the Council said, loud and clear, so that not only the people in church, but also everyone in the world could hear it: "Ecclesiastical Establishment" from now on you will be known again as, "The People of God."

For me, this felt like when the Lord changed the name of the People by having the prophet change the name of his illegitimate son from "Not-my-People" to "My People." Then the mantra of the Covenant would resonate in the hearts of the People again: "You are my People and I am your God."

Appropriately enough, "the People of God" isn't a completely new name. It's a golden oldie that is deeply rooted in the Hebrew and Christian scriptures and very emotionally charged for those who cherish it. By assuming it again as the name that best describes our community's contemporary self-understanding, we gave it new meaning and vitality in a modern context. By taking this name we said to the world, "This mysterious name symbolizes our deeply personal and pilgrim nature. It's who we really are." This gave us a way of re-minding ourselves of what all the prophetic reforms that followed the Council were all about. We would simply say, "We are the People of God," or, "We are a Pilgrim People," and just keep moving.

*The first thing we have to do
is to notice
that we've loaded down this camel
with so much baggage
we'll never get through the desert alive.
Something has to go....*

In a more modest but very personal way, the change of heart that our whole community was going through at the time was reflected for me in how the courses I was taking at the Gregorian University were stretching me in two directions toward a genuine theological renewal. In my first two years, my courses were taught mostly by elderly professors who had been teaching them for a very long time. In their teaching they followed the classical scholastic method of the early medieval period. In the hands of theological giants like Bonaventure, Thomas Aquinas, and Albert the Great, this method was initially fashioned and employed to expand the horizons of Christian understanding and to articulate a vision that integrated believing, understanding, and the cutting edge intellectual movements of medieval culture.

By the time I got to Rome, however, this method was tired out. It was being used to provide "proof texts" to refute certain doctrinal errors, especially those of the Protestant Reformers and the "Modernists." We were seldom, if ever, obliged to read the original works of the persons we were refuting. Basically, what we were expected to do was to memorize the theses, the arguments, and the texts that proved these Reformers wrong.

The whole scene changed in my third year at the Greg when a wave of younger teachers came there from all over the world. They brought with them a whole new modern approach to Augustine's classical "faith seeking understanding" which was much less argumentative and much more scientific, dialogical and process-oriented than what I had become accustomed to. These professors opened a window for me on a whole new way of theologizing.

Of course, the challenge that came with this open window is that it put me right in the middle of the tension between the window that had been closed for so long and the one that had just recently been opened. There I was, right in the middle, being stretched again. This time, I was being stretched between the classical and the contemporary way of understanding my faith.

For me, the immediate, practical implications of being stretched in this way were rather daunting. It meant that, in the oral examinations before graduation, I would not only have to be prepared to present and defend one hundred theses culled from my whole four years of theology—that would have been challenging enough. But I would also have to be prepared to present two quite different versions of these theses, depending on which group of professors I got as examiners. If the examining group happened to be mixed, I'd have an even greater challenge. I'd have to learn how to dance in Latin!

But it was worth it. It let me experience on a small scale how our whole Catholic community would be stretched by the change of heart we were about to experience in the Second Vatican Council.

Moving from Rome to Paris for my doctoral studies just before the Council opened felt to me like being personally stretched in a similar way. It felt like moving from the Church-centered City of Rome to the world-centered City of Paris.

I didn't tell anybody at the time but, paradoxically, I felt that I had become incurably anticlerical during the years I had spent in Rome. I wasn't militant about it, though. I just found Roman clericalism a bit hard to take with its tiresome pomp and circumstance, its primping and parading, its pretentious entitlement, and the flamboyant costumes that sometimes went with it.

"Remember one thing, Francis. You wouldn't have that collar if I didn't have this ring."

To me, the whole show seemed to belong to another age.

I may have thought I was anticlerical but, until I moved to Paris, I had no idea what it really meant to be anticlerical. Many of the French were professionals at it. They had been practicing it for centuries. And when the French have had enough of something, they've had enough of it. As a priest, I had more than one occasion to experience that.

When I arrived in a small mountain village in the south of France to replace the parish priest for a few months, many of the villagers there would pull their children off the street and close the shutters of their homes when they saw me coming. I felt like the Black Plague personified. There they were peeking at me fearfully from behind the closed shutters. And most of them were probably baptized Catholics, too.

I guess if a thoroughly clericalized community like ours is really going to reach out to the modern world, more of this kind of chastening experience will probably be a part of it. Anyway, I don't think I could have found a better place than Paris to start experiencing that.

For me, moving to Paris was like entering a whole new world. Everything was new: language, culture, experience of church, theology, ministering, a completely new experience of living alone, a whole new city to explore and learn from, without even mentioning the French cuisine that was totally new to me, as were the over two hundred types of French cheese. I wasn't taken by surprise by most of this though. I had foreseen that, in moving to Paris, I would be stretched a lot in this outward direction. Even though I found it intimidating at times, I welcomed this adventure.

Academically, however, I appeared to be heading in a whole other direction, as the thirty-some catechetical and community-organizing French students with whom I was boarding kept reminding me. I spent my four years in Paris alone with Augustine and Aquinas in a seventh floor, unheated garret getting to know them very personally. This experience stretched me more than I could ever have imagined. Although I learned a lot through it, it stretched me to the very edge of my capacities and endurance.

Even though, at the time, this was not a very popular direction in which to go, I never regretted it or felt obliged to apologize for it. It was clear to me that Augustine and Aquinas were the theologian's theologians in our Western Christian tradition. I figured that any time

I would spend rooting myself in these sources would be time well spent, no matter what I wound up doing. As I look back on it now, I believe that intuition has proven to be correct.

Early on, I got to know a German Benedictine monk who, of all things, was doing a *second* doctorate at the Sorbonne. He made a casual comment to me that proved to be very helpful. He said that doing a doctorate was not just about intelligence. If I weren't intelligent, I wouldn't be here. Doing a doctorate was about character. Did I have the character to see this through to the end? *That* was the key question.

He was right, too. Whether I had the character, or would be given the grace, to see this through to the end was *the* question for me every step of the way. It may have helped that I was studying what Augustine and Aquinas understood to be the Ultimate End of the human person. But, would I see this through to the end? *That* was the question.

I think that this is also *the* question our Catholic community has been living with for over forty years now. Ever since the Second Vatican Council envisioned us as a Pilgrim People blessed with a new heart and a new mind, we've been wondering "Do we have the character, or will we be given the grace, to see this pilgrimage through to the end?" We were very enthusiastic when we first headed out into this desert together. But after wandering around now for forty some years, going back to Egypt starts looking really good. Some of us are even tempted to resurrect an old idol or two. So, whether or not we can see this through to the end is really an open-ended question. It's as open as the window on the desert and the modern world that Pope (now Saint) John XXIII once had the courage to open for us even though he probably knew that he himself would never live to see the Promised Land.

As he left the final session of the Council, one of our leading Catholic theologians said that it would take us seventy-five years to realize what really had gone on there. Forty-five years later, that seems like a very modest estimate. We're just *beginning* to see that the desert the Reform has led us into is much bigger and much more challenging than we had ever imagined. Getting through this desert is going to take much more than character. It's going to take a completely new heart.

10

Living from the Easter Side

The real question is: What is worth investing a whole life in?
—Joseph Dorff, O. Praem. *We Are One in the Spirit.*

When he saw my brother Joe coming up the aisle that Sunday morning to celebrate the student Eucharist at Saint Norbert College, one of my former colleagues leaned over to his young son and whispered, "Father Dorff is going to say something very important today, Billy. Listen closely."

What my brother said was basically an enlargement on something very important that Jesus had said as he started and finished telling a parable in the Gospel for the day.

> *Avoid greed in all its forms....You fool! This very night your life will be required of you. To whom will all this piled-up wealth of yours go?*

Joe began his comments on this Gospel reading by saying,

> *In today's Gospel it wasn't Our Lord's point to scare His listeners with the threat of sudden death. The thought of a sudden death does in itself have a way of putting values back in perspective, and this is the point of His strong metaphor.*

At the heart of his homily, Father Joe added,

> *The question is not so much what should I invest in order to gain security—what should my portfolio look like, more bins for wheat for other stuff, or whatever? The real question is: What is worth investing a whole life in?*

After receiving the gifts of bread and wine from the people and offering them to God in thanksgiving and praise, Joe had a massive heart attack and fell dead at the altar. He was fifty-four years old.

The people present and the eight Norbertine priests who were concelebrating with Joe went into shock. They began wandering around the church aimlessly and then went home.

That was my brother's last Eucharist. It was left unfinished.

About three hours later I had also just finished celebrating the Eucharist at Holy Names College in Oakland where I was beginning a yearlong sabbatical. As I was making my thanksgiving after Mass, the sister superior asked if she could see me in the sacristy. She told me that Joe had died that morning while saying Mass. Then she and the other sisters made all the arrangements for me to fly back to our Abbey in Wisconsin to bury my brother. I'll never forget the kindness those sisters showed me on that day.

I probably should have guessed that, after his first heart attack, Joe knew that he only had two or three more years to live. I should have picked it up when he quoted Paul Goodman's "Little Te Deum" and passed a copy of the poem to me.

Little Te Deum

I'm not in pain, I owe no debts,
far as I know nobody hates
enough to harm me, no disgrace
tomorrow stares me in the face.

Far as I know no new disaster
is threatening my near and dear,
and I am less by nameless fears
beset than in my younger years

Thee God for this I therefore praise
interim of undesperate days

> *although it will not long endure.*
> *I do not live the various hour*
>
> *as the happy do or say:*
> *of homespun, of oatmeal gray,*
> *without a blazon is the flag*
> *that I hold up and do not wag.*

Joe treasured this little modern psalm. He said that it put just how he was feeling into words. I should have guessed that he was trying to tell me something else as well by giving me a copy of it, but I didn't. It was only in the reception line as we received Joe's body in the Abbey Church for Vespers that I learned that Joe had known all along that he only had a few more years to live. The heart surgeon who operated on him after his first heart attack told me.

With that, the radical change I had experienced over the past two years in Joe's relationship with me and with so many others began to make sense to me. I began to see very clearly how living with the threat of a sudden death had led Joe to put his own deepest values in perspective and then to put them into action. I began to see that, after his initial heart attack, Joe had been living these last few years from the other side of death. He had been living from the Easter Side.

In not telling me how long he had to live, Joe had honored one of our family's most sacrosanct canons. It was a canon that went very far back indeed.

"For God's sake, don't tell Francis," my mother would say, "It will upset him."

The remarkable thing about this inviolable canon was that it was universally applicable. We could apply it to everyone in the family just by changing the first name. Doing this wove us into a tightly knit family web of well-meaning secrecy and ignorance about what was really going on at a deeper level in one another's lives. Of course, we would always find some way of beating it. It just took us a little while. Toward the end of her life, my sister Catherine and I used to kid about how recklessly we disregarded this "not-telling canon" in our openhearted love for one another.

While he never told me how long he had to live, Joe did describe to me the very intimate after-death experience he had had on the operating table after his initial heart attack. As the good psychologist and meditative person that he was, Joe "monitored" very closely, both on the outside *and* on the inside, what he was experiencing in the operating room and took very good mental notes on it, as he always did. He told me,

> *All at once, I saw a very bright and beautiful Light shining up above me. I felt strongly attracted to the Light and spontaneously started moving toward it. Then I realized that I had left my body there on the operating table. From above, I could look down and see the doctors and nurses operating on me. My years of operating on monkey's brains as an experimental psychologist made me keenly aware of what was going on in the operation and that it was at a critical point.*
>
> *Still, as I watched it from above, I felt very peaceful. I felt strongly drawn to leave my body there on the operating table and to continue moving toward the welcoming Light.*
>
> *Then I heard one of the nurses saying, "Father, you can make it if you want to. You can make it."*
>
> *I then realized that I had a choice to make. If I wanted to, I could continue moving toward the Light. If I wanted to, I could return to my body. The choice was entirely mine.*
>
> *I waited a while.*
>
> *The nurse kept saying, "Father, you can make it, if you want to. You can make it."*
>
> *Then I decided to come back.*

I was with Joe every day in the week-long reentry that he made in the intensive care unit at Saint Vincent's Hospital. I would have to wait for an hour outside to be able to see him for three minutes. That's what I did for most of the day, all week long.

These three-minute meetings were a blessing. They didn't let us "solve all the problems of the world," as Joe and I were accustomed to doing whenever we would get together for any length of time. They just let us be deeply present to one another and let me assure Joe that we were all praying that he would make it.

The hours I spent in the waiting room gave me plenty of time to meditate. They didn't exactly let me put my values in perspective, though. I seemed to be at much too early a point in another major transition for that. What they did do, however, was to make me aware, in a way that I couldn't quite articulate, that some way or other I was sharing what Joe was experiencing. It was as though I was vicariously experiencing his brush with death. It was making all that I had been doing over the past ten years feel like so much straw. It was as though my life kept saying "vanity of vanities" to all of it and I was being called to leave it behind.

Strangely enough, this didn't upset me. It just made me feel that the rug had been pulled out from under me and the meaningfulness of all I had been doing with such great seriousness had gone with it. More and more, this vicarious death just felt like a matter of fact. It was how it was with me, that's all. It also made me grateful to Joe for it. I felt that, somehow or other, he was sharing this Easter Side experience with me. It was one of the many great gifts he gave me.

Meanwhile, Joe slowly regained his health and began to enjoy a strength and contentment that he hadn't known for quite a while. He also began to be much less inhibited than he usually had been in showing his affection for me and others. It felt as though, through this uninhibited loving-kindness, Joe was passing something on to me and that it had everything to do with the priesthood we shared. We never talked about this. It seemed that we didn't have to. We both seemed to realize it was going on.

I never really lived with Joe or knew him until I was thirty years old and joined him in teaching at Saint Norbert College. That may seem strange, but I think it goes with being the twelfth of thirteen children. I never knew my sister Cass until I started visiting her and her seven children. I never got to know Bill, and John, and Tom until they came back from the war. I never knew Jim at all. It was as though he went to the seminary when I was a baby and never returned. I guess that's one of the blessings of being from a large family. You can spend most of your lifetime getting to know your own brothers and sisters.

At any rate, during those five years in which we lived and taught together, Joe and I really made up for lost time. As my "big priest brother," with more talents than I could ever count, Joe was a wonderful mentor to me. As his "little priest brother," I was pretty much of a surprise to him. I imagine that I was a surprise that embarrassed him at times, but I also was a surprise that he greatly admired. I know that for sure because Cass told me so. Joe probably didn't tell me himself because he didn't want to "disturb" me.

When I first returned from Paris to join Joe on the faculty of Saint Norbert College, there were two important things that we didn't have in common. One was that Joe was a wonderful teacher and I was having a very painful and embarrassing year trying to "learn to teach by teaching." I was totally unprepared for this. It wasn't all that pleasant for my first students, either. They kept telling me that it was safe for me to land, whatever they meant by that. I think it may have had something to do with the fact that I thought I was still in graduate school and that they were graduate students. This landing image wasn't a bad image for what I was going through, though. My whole first year felt like I was an astronaut who had been in orbit for such a long time that some confreres began thinking that I never really existed. But here I was reentering the atmosphere from which I had graduated eight years earlier.

Joe was extremely supportive in guiding me through this yearlong reentry. As a professor of psychology, he had had a lot of experience working with space cadets. He was like my personal Mission Control Center.

One thing Joe said to me during this reentry experience was especially helpful. He said, "Fran, the luxury of being a student is that you can do your learning in private. The challenge of being a teacher is that you have to be willing to do your learning in public."

This really made sense to me. It let me articulate what the real question in all of this was and helped me wholeheartedly accept the challenge of doing the learning that I loved in public. The following year I joined Joe in being an effective teacher.

Another thing that Joe and I didn't have in common was our assessment of the recently completed Second Vatican Council. I was very enthusiastic about the vision it had articulated for the renewal of our community. I had already committed myself to helping implement it through the way I lived, and taught, and served.

Joe, on the other hand, had the strongest reservations about the Council. He based his assessment on the profound questions some seminarians were casually asking who had no intention of seriously addressing them, and on the often bizarre liturgical and religious "experiments" that were becoming popular on campus. As a scientist, Joe didn't find these "experiments" to be experiments at all, in any acceptable sense of that word that he knew. He found them to be fanciful, arbitrary, and without any reasonable or authoritative foundation he could discern. He was very distressed by what he experienced to be the lack of respect that these "questions" and "experiments" showed for the traditional faith that he treasured.

All of this changed for Joe when he was elected by the community to represent us at the worldwide Norbertine General Chapter of Renewal. Among the dedicated Norbertine men and scholars there, he discovered the logic of faith and the depth of the tradition and vision that animated the Second Vatican Council. He returned to the College advocating the spiritual renewal of our community with such quiet yet resolute conviction that it frightened many of us. But it didn't frighten me. It delighted me. Joe and I were now of one mind and one heart on teaching and living the wisdom of Vatican II.

At that time Joe and I were part of a community of about thirty Norbertine priests living together in the Priory on campus and teaching at the College. He was teaching experimental psychology and I was teaching philosophy and theology. I remember one of our community meetings in which we were discussing the renewal of the Order in preparation for our next international chapter of renewal. We were clearly getting nowhere. Finally, one of the theologians said, "I think we're talking about renewing the Order as though it were some big thing out there with no people in it. *We* are the Order here and now in this place. When we're talking about renewing the Order, we're talking about renewing the quality of how we're relating with one another."

That was a turning point in our discussion. It also was a turning point in the renewal of our local community. The turning point came with this shift in perspective from seeing the Order primarily as an institution to seeing it as a network of faithful relationships. With that we began talking about how we could renew an interpersonal "we," not an impersonal "it." As it did in the Council, this shift in emphasis from the institution to the People of God made all the difference in the world. The renewal we were seeking now became a question of openly turning toward one another in respectful dialogue, grassroots subsidiarity, and inclusive collegiality. These principles, which spiritually animated the Second Vatican Council, now began to animate our personal and communal renewal. It was a very exciting time to be alive.

Joe never really did tell me why he had decided to come back from his brush with death. I know he agreed with me that this was a very exciting time to be alive and maybe that had something to do with it. But maybe he just wanted to continue celebrating the intensified sense of friendship that characterized the last few years of his life. After all, he did introduce his final homily by saying,

> *...I noticed on a small Hallmark pocket calendar for this year that today, August 4, is Friendship Day. It's a nice warm feeling, even if it's not very widely observed, to have a day set aside on which to give thanks for the wonderful gift of friendship—for the benevolent, undemanding love of good friends over a lifetime; for the durable, timeless quality of friendship that neither the passage of years, nor distance, nor anything else that I have been able to discover, can destroy.*

But maybe he decided to come back so that he could spend a few more years in intensified thanksgiving and in praise. I remember him telling me how he would watch, as a watchman waits for dawn, so that he could praise God for the moment when the light rose from the darkness. He also described to me how he would touch his forehead to the floor each morning in thanksgiving for the gift of another day. And one of his favorite Psalms in those final few years was Psalm 139,

> ...*Truly you have formed my inmost being;*
> *you knit me in my mother's womb.*
> *I give you thanks that I am fearfully,*
> *wonderfully made...*

Joe ended his last homily by saying, "...in thanksgiving and praise."

I also know that in Buddhism the Compassionate Ones vow to come back from their experience of enlightenment until every single sentient being can accompany them into enlightenment. Maybe Joe had something like that in mind.

But from a purely personal point of view, I think Joe decided to come back so that he could let me feel and experience first-hand what it's really like to live life *here and now* from the Easter Side. I think he came back so that he could personally pass on to me the mantle of a very different kind of priesthood. I know he did, because I'm wearing that mantle now. It's not a *cappa magna*. It's not an ornate cope or a new chasuble. It's not the emblazoned cape of an evangelizing crusader. It's the homespun, woolen, oatmeal gray robe of a wandering pilgrim. It reminds me very much of the robe Norbert wore as a wandering peacemaker. As I wear this robe I realize that Joe is much more than a faithful confrere, a gifted colleague, a dear friend, and a blood brother to me. He's my priest.

After we buried Joe and all the guests had gone home, I flew back to California to continue what would be one the happiest years of my life, my sabbatical at the University in Berkeley.

No one could see him, of course, but Joe came with me. We spent the whole year together. And he's still with me. We're even closer now than we were on those Friday nights after a week of teaching when we would go out with a few good Norbertine friends to have a beer and a pizza and to solve all the problems of the world.

11

Who Closed the Classroom Door?

> *Ecclesiastes suggests, maybe a job isn't worth pouring our whole life into and shutting everything else out. Not worth it often; as we find in the emptiness of some lives upon retirement when the whole meaning of life seems to disappear with the job description.*
> —Joseph Dorff, O. Praem., We Are One in the Spirit.

After a shaky start, I really began to hit my stride in teaching college theology. For the first seven years things just seemed to be getting better and better. I responded by dedicating myself totally to my college teaching by giving it a hundred and twenty percent of my energy.

Why not? I loved the challenge of seeking Wisdom side-by-side with some very gifted students who were searching for something more, just as I was. I enjoyed the enriching company of colleagues with backgrounds much different than mine, and the inter-disciplinary teaching I did with many of them. I felt blessed not only by being able to meet with students and colleagues in the classroom, but also, as a college chaplain, by being able to lead them and their families in the renewed liturgy of Vatican II. It couldn't have been better. I thought that, after so much demanding preparation, I had finally found my lifetime niche in the college classroom. Then the classroom door slammed shut.

At first, "Who closed the classroom door?" wasn't even a question in my mind. It was very clear to me who had closed the classroom door. I felt that the young, newly-appointed president had slammed it in my face by not granting me tenure. Before I let her know that in no uncertain terms, I laced up my combat boots and began stomping around the campus. It wasn't a pretty sight. But that didn't bother me at all. I was hurting so bad and kicking up so much dust I couldn't even see it. To me, it felt as if, for several years, I had been going a hundred and fifty miles an hour straight ahead, giving it all I had, and then, all of a sudden, someone had thrown my life in reverse and stripped the gears. I didn't see it coming, and I couldn't see behind me at all. The only option I seemed to have was to jump out in protest and stomp around the campus in my combat boots.

I may have lost my vision but the gifted young president hadn't lost hers. Despite the financial crunch the college was going through, she managed to invite me to stay on by piecing together three part-time positions for me: part-time chaplain, part-time teacher, and part-time assistant to the president for strategic planning. Her gracious gesture finally let me see how stupid I look and sound and feel stomping around in combat boots. It let me take my boots off again and humbly apologize to her. I decided to show that I really meant it, too, by throwing myself totally into the strategic planning that might help her lead the College to better times. I figured that this would give me two good years to do my best to continue implementing the reforms of Vatican II on campus, and to help transform the painfully ugly ending I had created into a cordially gracious one.

I knew right from the beginning, however, that I would have to leave the college after that. Besides breaking my nose, the closing of the classroom door had broken my heart. It had radically shaken my commitment to teaching in a Catholic college and raised all kinds of unanswered questions about what I was to do with my life. I felt that, no matter what happened, it would never be the same again. The consoling thing that I had learned from this most embarrassing experience was that Rosemont College had been blessed with a very good president and that it was a privilege to work with her. So I put my teaching shoes on again and went back into the classroom for the time being.

It was shortly after this that my brother Joe suffered his first heart attack. That was another great blow for me. It thoroughly shook me up and took me from the classroom to a long vigil in the intensive care unit. In a much deeper way, it brought into question all that I had been doing with my life.

So, then, "Who closed the classroom door?"

My deeper answer to this question was a lot more honest and hit much closer to home. I did. I closed it without even noticing that

I had closed it. I closed it by overworking my way to burnout. Even after the president opened it again for me, I continued closing it in this way until I developed a serious arthritic condition in my neck, and my health began to give out. That finally became clear to me when my doctor wrote out a prescription for a pain killer for me and told me that I was to take these pills twice a day and that I wouldn't have to see him again.

"You mean I just have to take these pills for the rest of my life?" I asked.

"Yes," the doctor replied.

I knew there must be a better option than that. That's when I finally decided to take a leave of absence from the classroom and to take time to pay much more attention to my body.

I had tried to convince the Abbot the year before that I was run down and needed a break, but he answered, as a lot of religious superiors are inclined to do, by encouraging me just to "hang in there." "You're doing a fine job," he said, "and, besides, there isn't anyone to replace you."

As the Abbot said this I could hear the familiar strains of our old marching song playing loudly in the background, "We die with our boots on around here." And I had even brought colored markers and some drawing paper to the meeting to let the Abbot see my problem in living color! I actually drew him a picture of me holding three balloons, or jobs, from the time I had first arrived at the Abbey a few years earlier. That went to four balloons the next year, six the following year, and here I am now, I said, trying to keep eight different balloons in the air at the same time.

I thought that this picture would really do it, but the Abbot just looked at me quizzically and asked, "Now what in the world are you drawing balloons for, Fran?"

The penny dropped for him two years later when I went to him and simply said, "John, I'm burned out."

"Burned out?" he said. "You need to get away."

Precisely. It just took me two years to find the right word for it, that's all. This made me realize once and for all that, when you're in transition, as I often am, having the right word for it is very important.

Another example of this was when I followed up on my conversation with the Abbot by taking a leave of absence from Rosemont College. At first, when my colleagues would ask me, "Fran, what are you doing next year?" I'd reply by saying, "I'm taking a leave of absence."

"A leave of absence?" they'd respond with a look of such grave concern on their faces that it made me feel as though I had just contracted a fatal disease that was contagious.

"Wrong word," I thought to myself.

So, when the next colleague asked me, "Fran, what are you doing next year?" I replied. "I'm taking a sabbatical."

"A sabbatical," he said with evident approval, "congratulations."

"Right word," I thought to myself.

But what was I actually doing the following year? No matter what we called it, I was doing the same darn thing. I was getting off the scene so that no one who knew me could see that I didn't know what I was doing the next year.

On a much deeper level still, God closed the classroom door. God did it by continually calling me to a much more contemplative way of living, to a different rhythm in my life, and to a very different kind of teaching. The way I look at it, since I was much too busy to pick up the subtle suggestions through which God was trying to point me in this direction, God just slammed the classroom door in my face so that I'd at least start to get the message.

I never told the president of the College this, but that means that both she, and my burning out, were instruments of God's will for me. "O happy fault!" as we sing in the liturgy during the Easter Vigil. But, in this case, I would have to keep a long vigil trying to kick the classroom door open again with my combat boots before I'd really learn to sing "O happy fault!" with real conviction.

My year in Berkeley restored my health and spirits, gave me time to meditate again, renewed my sense of wonder at the awesome beauty of nature, immeasurably enriched my life, and got me back into good physical shape. It was one of the happiest years of my life.

All of which made me think that I was ready and able to go back into the classroom again. So I accepted positions as an Assistant Professor of theology at the Catholic Theological Union in Chicago; as the Director of Formation for our community's students of theology, a position my brother Joe had been assigned to take before he died; and as Superior of our House of Studies. I also began training in spiritual direction. That's four big balloons right from the start! Not a good omen.

In returning to the classroom, I was surprised to find that I had lost my confidence as a teacher. Even though the students didn't seem to notice, I felt that things weren't going well at all. I would sit up half the night anxiously preparing a lecture that would usually have taken me an hour or two to prepare. At the same time a fundamental assumption of mine began to shift. I had been assuming that the young seminarians were our future and that it was best to focus all of my energy for implementing the reform of Vatican II on their initial formation. While I still thought that may be true in the long run, I began to think that many of the seminarians were much too young and inexperienced to lead the reform movement at this critically important time. Ministerially, they were still very wet behind the ears, as I had been at their age. I thought that, if they were going to lead a Pilgrim People through the desert, they would have to spend a lot more time in the desert themselves, just as Moses did. Although I personally was experiencing the seminary as a desert of a sort, that isn't exactly the kind of desert I had in mind.

I began to think that the renewal of Vatican II would in fact be led by those seasoned ministers who had borne the day's heat and hadn't left when the changes that came with it opened the doors. I knew that these dedicated women and men had hash marks on their hearts from all the changes they had come through. But there they were, still selflessly helping their people. I began to see them as the ones who could lead our Pilgrim People through the desert. These were the older students I was teaching in the summer institutes of renewal at Saint Norbert College. They were students who were ready and waiting to hear the Good News in a way that rang true to them. This fundamental shift in my vision and interest didn't do much at all to improve the teaching I was doing in the seminary. It only helped make me feel more out of place in the classroom.

As scary as it was for me even to entertain, it was time for me to admit that the classroom door had closed for me years ago, and to stop pretending that it was still as open as it had been for so long. It was time for me to let go of the teaching that I thought would be my lifework and see what would happen then. It was time for me to begin praying "Thy will be done" and actually mean it.

I didn't find any of these options to be especially attractive. But I knew for sure that, if God really had closed the door to the classroom, it would be fruitless for me to try to pry it open again. Forget about that.

It would be a very long four years in Chicago.

12

Letting My Life Be Wise

Of all the things I've said and done
may I be known for this alone:
for letting my life be wise.

—Ira Progoff *(a paraphrase)*

What a treat it was to hear Joseph Campbell and Ira Progoff in dialogue for a whole day on the topic of Myth and Spirit. The dialogue was hosted by an Anglican community in Cleveland, Ohio, and took place in their beautiful Gothic church. At the time, Campbell and Progoff were two pioneers in the field of psyche and symbol at the peak of their careers. The church was packed.

The longer the dialogue went on, however, the more intricate, complex, and theoretical it seemed to become. It was good to hear these two giants conversing in this way with such evident respect for one another, but to be able to keep up with what they were saying was something else.

After the day-long dialogue was finished, the crowd went home and Ira Progoff led a group of about twenty-five of us to the crypt of the church to begin a weekend retreat in the Intensive Journal Method.

I found our moving from the heady discussion in the worship space above to the meditative work in the crypt below to be a very symbolic journey in itself. It symbolized for me the journey I had been making over the previous five years from talking *about* religious experience in the classroom to exploring my own spiritual experience in deep meditation. It also symbolized for me what Ira's lifework was really all about. It was all about finding our way to the deep place within us from which all the dogmas, teachings, rituals, symbols, classrooms, and cathedrals on the surface of our lives come, and experiencing for ourselves what goes on in that deep place.

A day later, as some of the participants began to read aloud from what they had personally experienced in the meditation of the wellspring beneath the cathedral, I could feel the cathedral's foundations beginning to shake with new spiritual energy and to settle into a much deeper place. We were *experiencing* in the crypt what Campbell and Progoff had been *talking about* the day before in the church. More importantly for me, we were experiencing in the crypt what I had only been *talking about* for fifteen years in the classroom. Ira would often summarize this difference by saying that what we need in today's culture is not more information about spiritual experience but an undeniable personal experience of the spiritual dimension of our lives. He summarized the journey this entails even more powerfully for me when he concluded one of his Entrance Meditations, *The Well and the Cathedral*, with these words,

> *...Since that time*
> *many have come to the cathedral*
> *to pay their respects,*
> *to praise the name of their god,*
> *to ask favors of many kinds.*
> *They all seem to know*
> *that something important is there,*
> *that something important is present*
> *at the site of the cathedral.*
>
> *The well*
> *that leads to the underground stream*
> *is at the base of the cathedral.*
> *But now it is covered by stones*
> *and difficult to find.*
>
> *How shall we get to the well*
> *now that it has been covered*
> *by the stones of the cathedral,*
> *now that it has been hidden*

*by the passage
of the centuries?*

*We have found a way.
We can go there together.
There is a shaft of a well
beneath the cathedral.
And where is the cathedral?
We have nowhere to look
and nowhere to go,
for you are the cathedral,
I am the cathedral.
The way to the underground stream
is the well
that is hidden within us....*

  This weekend retreat was by no means my first contact with Ira Progoff's creative work of meditatively evoking—rather than rationally analyzing—the psyche. By this time Ira and I were good friends and had been collaborating in this work for several years. Ever since my first workshop with him about five years earlier, I had taken his Intensive Journal Method as my primary form of meditative practice. Shortly after that, I spent a post-doctoral year with his assistance, studying his approach to creative and spiritual growth and comparing it to other major systems in developmental psychology. Without saying it, what I was doing in all of this was seeing whether or not Ira's was the holistic method of seeking Wisdom that would let me do my theologizing in a much broader and deeper way than I had been doing. By year's end, I had unequivocally decided that it was.

  This was a very creative time in Ira's life. Integrating insights were coming to him so fast that he couldn't keep up with them. When that would happen to Jung, Ira said that Jung would lie down on the floor, let the ideas fly out the window, then get up, look out the window, and peacefully write down whatever ideas he could still see.

When Ira would have a similar experience of creative overload at this time, which could be about three or four times a week, he'd call me from New York and we'd explore the new ideas. These long telephone conversations greatly enriched and energized my life and my research. At this time his work was also generating national interest, especially among the Catholic community for whom it provided a congenial tool for working through the major personal, communal, and spiritual changes that had been occasioned by the Second Vatican Council.

It was during my post-doctoral year that Ira invited me to join him as his first consultant in offering the Intensive Journal workshops nationwide. He did this in a rather brusque but, nevertheless, very effective way. He had originally promised to make his unpublished manuscripts and correspondence available to me once I had finished studying all that he had published. When I eventually asked him for the manuscript material, he refused to respond or to make it available to me. We carried on this sort of cat-and-mouse exchange for a couple of months until I finally met with him personally about it at a workshop that he was giving at the University of Chicago.

He was clearly upset. "You can write your damn six volume German study of my intellectual development after I die," he said. "If you want to work with me, then you have to give the workshops."

"Okay," I said. "That sounds good to me."

So I gave up my study of his work and joined him in non-analytically teaching his approach to psychological and spiritual development through the Intensive Journal. It wasn't long before I was leading about fifteen workshops a year.

As I see it now, this marked a major turning point in my life. It coincided with the four years in Chicago during which I was being forced to admit, whether I liked it or not, that the classroom door had definitively closed for me. At the same time, it opened up for me a much deeper, non-directive, evocative way of teaching spiritually. It was solidly grounded in the thirty years of research and experimentation that Ira had devoted to creating and developing a comprehensive method for a contemporary holistic depth psychology.

Ira was clearly delighted to have me as a collaborator and friend in the next phase of his work. I was just as delighted to have him as a friend and mentor during what was one of the most disorienting, challenging, and creative transitions I've ever made. It was a most creative time for both of us.

Six months before I ever met him personally, I met Ira in one of the most extraordinary of his many extraordinary books. I was visiting a friend who had a stack of unread books on his desk. He invited me to browse through them and let him know if I came across anything that was worth reading.

That night, I opened Ira's book, *The Symbolic and the Real*. It was the third in a trilogy of books in which he had clearly outlined the whole development of modern psychology with the intention of discerning the next step it called for and then taking it. The book opened with a description of Socrates' evocative method of teaching which called forth from the soul of a student the wisdom that was already there in an unrealized and unarticulated way. It then suggested what a modern psychology would look like that employed a similar evocative method, rather than a cognitively analytic and didactic one, and how that would give us access once again to the empirical reality of our own symbolic experiences. We would then recognize symbols not as "just symbols," but as extremely important, legitimate, and revelatory channels of a deeper kind of knowing.

That meant that we would have two kinds of empiricism and two kinds of science. One would be an outer empiricism and a science of external experience with an analytic method of study and verification. It would be focused on the objective world of "it" and "its." The other would be an inner empiricism and a science of internal experience with a descriptive and evocative method of study and verification. It would be focused on the subjective world of "I" and "we." This second empiricism would put us in touch once again with the *reality* of the symbols that energize and animate our lives. It would let us document through personal experience that the symbolic is *real*. In a culture that was and still is radically out of touch with the symbolic dimension of life, this would represent a quiet revolution of the first order. I was so energized by Ira's vision of the symbolic and the real that I could hardly sleep. I guess I should have gotten up with notebook in hand and looked out the window.

What got me so excited was that, in *The Symbolic and the Real,* Ira Progoff was describing exactly what I had been looking for ever since the classroom door had slammed shut in my face. It made me realize that an important part of the difficulties I was experiencing in the classroom was that I was becoming increasingly dissatisfied and frustrated with the very real limitations of the cognitive approach to spiritual experience which was the only one I knew that was acceptable in academic circles. At the time, the trouble was that I didn't have a clear vision of what a viable alternative to the academic perspective might be, and I had no idea of what would be an effective methodology to explore and communicate it. I realized that part of the difficulty I was having in teaching was that I was trying to work this out in the classroom and it clearly wasn't working. *The Symbolic and the Real* showed me that Ira Progoff had been living and working for thirty years with these two questions about a viable alternative to the analytic perspective and method. He subsequently developed the *Intensive Journal* Method of creative and spiritual growth as a way of actively answering them.

The next morning I put his copy of *The Symbolic and the Real* on my friend's desk and said, "Joel, we have to go to one of these workshops." A few months later, on Pentecost weekend, we both showed up for an *Intensive Journal* workshop at the South Side Cenacle Retreat House in Chicago. When the janitor finally stopped wandering around, rearranging chairs, and testing the sound system, he sat down in the front of the hall and said, "Well, let's get started." I realized then that he wasn't the janitor at all! He was Ira Progoff. From then on, the sparks started flying for me. It was a great way to celebrate the feast of Pentecost.

What a gift this first meeting turned out to be. An important part of it was that I saw Ira modeling for me the way I felt that I was being called to teach. He wasn't lecturing or giving us something else to think about. He was leading us in a meditative process that let each of us get in touch with what was going on within us. Then he would listen to what we said—more deeply than most of us were able to—and suggest how we might take the next step in exploring the unfolding wisdom of what our life really wanted to become.

Over the next few years I made close to twenty workshops and retreats under Ira's direction. In all of these, I never saw him violate the evocative method of teaching that he was modeling for us. What a gift a teacher of this quality was for me.

As a young man passionately interested in the search for Wisdom no matter what form it took, Ira found in the work of C.G. Jung the sense of depth and historical development that he had been looking for. So he decided to do his doctoral dissertation on the social implications of Jung's psychology. The trouble was that, at that time, he couldn't find any psychology department in this country that would accept a thesis on Jung's work. So he had to do his doctorate on Jung in the history of ideas at the New School of Social Research in New York. When Jung and the Bollingen Foundation saw the quality of Ira's work, they invited him to come to Switzerland to study personally with Jung for three years.

At his first meeting with Jung, Ira introduced himself by telling Jung that he had begun the defense of his dissertation by saying, "In this defense I will attempt to demonstrate that C.G. Jung is not a Jungian."

Jung pushed his glasses up onto his forehead, as he often would when something touched him deeply, leaned back in his chair, and silently stared at the ceiling for a moment. Then he straightened up, looked at Ira and said, "That's right. I'm *not* a Jungian. I never was a Jungian. And I never will be a Jungian."

Going out on a limb, Ira said, "Well, if you're not a Jungian, then why do you let your friends at the Jungian Institute here teach you as though you were a Jungian?"

"If my friends don't teach me as a Jungian," Jung quipped, "my enemies will. So I let my friends do it."

Taking the dialogue a step further, Ira asked, "But if you had it your way, how would you want your work to be taught?"

Jung thought for a moment and then smiled. "It would be too strange," he said. "It would be a modern psychology with a touch of Zen."

I don't know how long that conundrum stayed with Ira but I know it initially struck him as a koan that he was called to meditate on. "What *would* 'a modern psychology with a touch of Zen' look like?" Perhaps that's what led him to study with D.T. Suzuki when he returned home, and to later write *The Well and the Cathedral* and two other very evocative books of entrance meditations as an integral part of his *Intensive Journal* Method. At any rate, the holistic depth psychology that Ira himself eventually developed was clearly "a modern psychology with a touch of Zen." In more ways than one, he had taken Jung's work a giant step further."

One of Ira's personal mantras was "Out of the silence it comes." I could see by the way he taught and worked that much of his new psychology was coming out of his own meditative silence. A very big part of our *Intensive Journal* work was spent in being "alone and yet together" in the silence. All of our formal meditative work began with the phrase, "In the Silence....In the Silence...."

My last meeting with Ira was a lunch at the Vallombrosa Retreat Center in California during what was to be his final workshop. Because of his weakened condition, due to the disease of progressive supranuclear palsy, we spent the whole meal just sitting together, smiling at one another in the silence. I have since heard that Hindus sometimes honor a spiritual master in that way. They simply sit with him in the silence. It seemed very appropriate to me that I was able to honor the importance of Ira's presence in my life in the very same way.

I once asked Ira how I could tell when I was ready to join him in teaching this work. He answered right away, "If you have something very important to tell others that you think will make a great difference in their lives, you're not ready for this work." This comment still helps me remember that this work is one of spiritual indirection. How masterfully Ira had modeled this for me at a critically important time in my life.

I think what Ira said of C.G. Jung as he began the defense of his doctoral dissertation can now be said of him as well. Ira Progoff is not a "Jungian." He's also not a "Progoffian." His lifework was not about joining a school of psychology or advocating or elaborating a psychological system. Nor was it about trying to provide final answers to the perennial questions that each of our lives raise. His lifework was about letting our life become wise by developing the meditative sensitivity to notice how it is moving and how to follow that animating movement.

In the Silence….In the Silence….

Ira's life ended in this meditative silence. His debilitating condition gradually took away his ability to speak and his muscular control. In the end, it led him silently to the Source of the wisdom that was his.

Of all the things I've said and done
may I be known for this alone:
for letting my life be wise.

13

Living in the In-between

*We do not find meaning in things nor do we put it into things,
but between us and things it can happen.*
—Martin Buber, *Between Man and Man*

I'm saying good-bye to Ira as I leave his home which is one of those stately old buildings on Woodlawn Avenue near the University of Chicago. His brother is in the parlor with us. Ira offers to take me home in his horse-drawn carriage. At first I say that won't be necessary since it isn't far for me to walk to Holy Spirit Priory where I'm living. However, when Ira insists, I say I'd enjoy that. Somehow or other, I can see that his brother doesn't want Ira to take me home. Ira says that he'll be ready in a minute. Then he goes upstairs to say goodbye to his wife. I don't know why but I feel an anima-laden atmosphere in the house at this time that I associate with Ira's wife upstairs.

We climb into his old open carriage and Ira begins to drive me down Woodlawn Avenue toward home. Halfway there, I'm surprised to see a majestic old Gothic Monastery on the left-hand side of the street. The building is large, imposing, and silent. I don't see any sign of life around it at all; no monks, no other people.

By contrast, on the right-hand side I see the great stone buildings of an old University that is full of life. The buildings are literally overflowing with students who are having a lot of fun screaming and yelling as they jump out the windows and climb down the walls of the University like a troop of monkeys.

Our carriage moves peacefully up the street between the Monastery and the University on our way home. Then I wake up.

This dream came to me during my second year of working with Ira Progoff. At that time, I was living in Chicago and was right in the middle of a major transition from academic to spiritual teaching. When I enthusiastically read this dream to Ira, his only reaction was, "I don't have a brother."

Of course, for me, this dream wasn't about whether or not Ira had a brother. It was about my finding a pathway that would lead me home at a time when my life seemed stuck. The dream intimated that it would not be a pathway that would lead me to yet another University or Monastery, but one that would lead me *in-between* these two important institutions that have shaped my whole adult life.

As is often the case with "big dreams" like this, this dream came before its time. I was still working through a very confusing and painful time of transition while trying to cling to the classroom, which only made things more confusing and painful. I was also beginning to show signs of the wear and tear this was taking on me by how terribly short-tempered and angry I was getting to be. It was clearly "combat boots time" again for me, even though I thought my previous transition had taught me the fine art of "graceful endings" once and for all.

In the middle of all of this, this dream came to me like a message from heaven. I felt it was giving me a glimpse of a possible future and the glimmer of hope that goes with it. Things may not have been moving on the surface of my life but, as the dream assured me, they were already moving within me.

This dream led me in two directions. In anticipating, it took me into the future; in re-membering, it took me deep within my past. It took me once again to all the monasteries, cathedrals, and universities in this country and in Europe which I have visited or in which I have lived, studied, or taught. It let me experience again the beauty of these special places of Wisdom and understanding and how much I love them and have learned from them. It also made me conscious of how I still collect monasteries and universities. Whenever I'm in an area where there is a monastery or a university, I make it a point to visit it, to walk its campus, and to savor the atmosphere of this special place. This dream carried that same atmosphere of admiration and indebtedness.

That in itself would have been a lot, but it wasn't all this dream gave me. It gave me a deeply moving dream-symbol that summed up for me practically a lifetime of commuting back and forth from Monastery to University, from altar to classroom, from priest to professor.

This image reflected both the desire for God and the love of learning which have animated my whole adult life. It also put me in touch again with my mentor, Thomas Aquinas, and how this monk-scholar lived and articulated for all time a marvelous integration of the competing monastic and university ways of knowing. I believe he was able to do this by having the courage and intelligence to do his theologizing *in-between* these two powerful movements in medieval culture. He did it by having the courage to take the road less traveled that passes *in-between* the Monastery and the University, and in-between the many disputed questions that kept threatening to divide the Christian world into armed camps.

In putting me in touch with Aquinas again, this dream also conjured up a scene that has always moved me deeply. It let me see Albert the Great as an old man, making the long journey all the way from Cologne to Paris to defend the memory of his most gifted student against a posthumous accusation of heresy. Saint Thomas Aquinas being considered, not only as a misfit, but also as a heretic! That goes against practically all the press Thomas is currently getting.

I don't blame Thomas for making me a misfit, though. I wasn't even thinking of him in those terms at the time. I knew that he had taught me not just to mouth *what* he thought but to imitate *how* he thought. He didn't just teach me theology. He taught me how to theologize by having the courage to live, believe, and think *in-between* us and God and all the positions and counter-positions I would experience along the way. This kind of theologizing fit my innate love of learning and my desire for God to a "T."

However, as I tried to remain faithful to Thomas's approach, I found that, even in the monastery and the university, the *in-between* was not common ground. In fact, it was very uncommon ground. If I kept believing, living, and thinking from this position, it meant I couldn't join the crowd. It meant I couldn't even join the club. For me, living in the *in-between* became the road less traveled. That's where being a misfit finally began to come in, whether I had a name for it or not. It came on the road less traveled. I don't think that living in the *in-between* is the only path to being a misfit but, it was—and still is—a privileged one for me.

I didn't have the presence of mind at the time—perhaps I was too young—but I could have very appropriately opened the defense of my dissertation on Aquinas' theologizing just as Ira had opened his on Jung. I could have introduced it by saying, "In this presentation I intend to defend the proposition that Thomas Aquinas is not a "Thomist," while adding under my breath, "and neither am I." Whether I had the presence of mind to say it at that time or not, the important thing is that that's how it turned out for me.

I remember once applying for a teaching position at a small Catholic college. I started having questions about it right away when I wasn't asked to meet with the Dean, the Department Chairperson, or any of the faculty. I was led right to the President's office for the interview. I started having even more questions about it when the sister who was president began the interview by asking, "Well, Father, are you way in or way out?"

"Well, Sister," I candidly replied without even thinking about it, "to those who are way out, I seem to be way in, and to those who are way in, I seem to be way out." That's really how it was with me. After the interview, Sister offered me the teaching position but, for some reason or other, I politely declined.

I didn't fare much better when I was invited for an interview with the chairperson of the philosophy department of a prestigious university. I suggested that I might be able to fill the gap I saw in their offerings in the area of medieval philosophy in general, and in the thought of Augustine, Bonaventure, and Aquinas in particular. But to everything I said, the chairperson kept replying, "But we teach language analysis here."

In reply, I finally said that I hadn't realized that this was a department of linguistic analysis. I thought it was a department of philosophy, of the art of falling in love with Wisdom. This must have seemed like a thoroughly jaded, even medieval, perspective, since I wasn't offered the position. I think it was just as well. I had very little background or interest in linguistic analysis and none at all in substituting it for "the love of Wisdom."

To return to my dream, it struck me as significant that it portrayed Ira and me as *traveling* between the monastery and the university not just *standing* between them, since I've never experienced the *in-between* as a static space. For me it has always been a dynamic, highly-charged space with creative tension pulling me in four directions. The tug-of-war that's going on there is between two opposing poles and between past forms and future perspectives which promise to be more expansive and all-embracing, even though they still are slightly beyond my current horizon. The fact that my dream also pictured Ira and me moving *peacefully* through such a highly-charged space was no small consolation to me at the time.

It was immediately clear to me that the old carriage in the dream symbolized the vehicle of Ira's holistic depth psychologizing that we both recognized was a work that was bigger than both of us and that we were privileged to share. Previously, many different sources had helped me clarify and articulate my personal experience of living in the *in-between*. Among these were the dynamics of the biblical Exodus and Passover experiences; my experience of either-or thinking as a depersonalizing dead-end; the depth of the both-and perspective of Taoist thinking; the non-dual perspective of Hindu and Christian mystics; and Martin Buber's remarkably creative life and practice of personalizing dialogue.

In my courses in theology, I think I eventually became quite effective in communicating to my students the nature and importance of living in the *in-between*. Deep down, that's what I understand believing to be all about. It's not just about this *or* that. It's certainly not just about this *against* that. It's about finding a way of embracing and transcending all the seeming contradictions of life: faith and understanding; nature and grace; belief and doubt, not knowing and knowing, light and darkness; charism and institution; individual and community; monastery and university; joy and pain; life and death. No wonder I find the *in-between* of faith to be such a highly-charged space.

However, for the most part, the way in which I was able to

communicate this understanding in the classroom remained largely notional, for my students *and* for me. I had not yet developed the kind of meditative practice and the symbolizing sensitivity that would help me, not just to *advocate* living in the *in-between*, but actually to *share and evoke* the experience of it in others. Developing that capacity was an important part of my being able to move gracefully from the classroom to the retreat house, from teaching academically to teaching spiritually.

That's precisely what my internalizing Ira's lifework enabled me to do. It gave me a comprehensive perspective and a meditative method, a practice and tool for working with every aspect of life's self-integrating movement. The deceptively simple meditative exercises he had experimentally developed in person-to-person dialoguing and in embracing the polarities of life's conundrums helped me to experience and share living in the *in-between* not just as a good idea but as an animating lifework. After walking barefoot for such a long time, this was a carriage I was greatly relieved to climb into.

However, even after I was quite experienced in this meditative practice, it took me a long time to come up with an actual image or two that might communicate and evoke the experience of living in the *in-between* for retreatants and spiritual seekers. Once, when I was puzzling about this after a session in which I had dismally failed to communicate the experience, I came across a life-size *santo* of St. Francis standing in prayer just outside the retreat house door. He was peacefully holding his hands out to me. In-between his hands, was a small, empty space.

"That's it!" I thought. "That's the image! On the one hand, this. On the other hand, that. And in-between, a highly-charged space that seems to be empty. That's it! There's an invisible energy field moving through the empty space between his hands."

In the very next retreat, I presented this image as a symbol of how our lifeline moves through a highly-charged energy field as it weaves its way through the two sides of our story, whatever they may be at a given time. I tried to symbolize this by asking one of the sisters to extend her hands just as I had seen the statue of Francis doing. I asked her not to bring her palms together with no space *in-between*, as we usually do in prayer. I also asked her not to clench her fists, as we often do when we're fighting life. I asked her just to imitate Francis as I had experienced him at the doorway by reaching out toward me with an empty, non-possessive space between her outstretched hands. It was as though, on the one hand, was the good news. On the other hand, was the bad news. And, in the empty space between them was the invisible dialoguing that kept her hands facing one another.

As she stood there with hands outstretched, I began to pass my hand between hers to symbolize the lifeline of dialogue moving through the empty space *in-between* her hands. Then suddenly—zap!—both of us were surprised by a charge of electrostatic energy.

"Did you feel that?" I asked, as I pulled my hand away.

"Yes!" she said, wondering what had happened.

"I promise, I'll never do it again," I joked as the class broke out laughing.

But, of course, I *would* do it again. It had let the retreatants see for themselves how highly charged living in the *in-between* can be. While they were laughing at my silly demonstration, I could hear a very important penny drop.

In a later retreat session I turned to music to try to communicate symbolically the dynamics of living in the *in-between*. At the end of a week-long retreat, I had the participants break up into three choirs in an effort to concretize and summarize all that we had explored in our meditations and reflections on *LifeProcess*. The three choirs were the "good news choir," the "bad news choir," and the "*in-between* choir."

First, I started the good news choir off continually singing a verse from the *Magnificat* in a major key as a solo treble line:

"*The Lord has done marvels for me...*"

Then, I led the bad news choir in countering this joyful song with a bass line by repeatedly singing a phrase from a Psalm in a minor key:

"*In my trouble and distress...*"

With this dissident duet firmly established, I brought in the

in-between choir singing, in a *fortissimo* middle voice like a chorus of Bach trumpets, the Pauline phrase,
 "*Glory be to God whose power working in us...*"

And there we were, a pilgrim chorus singing a cacophonous trio from within the experience of living in the *in-between*.

I tried to conduct this chorus to a dramatically abrupt close but the retreatants just kept on singing. They were having too much fun. They were singing and laughing and listening and looking at each other as if to say, "What in the world's going on here?" They couldn't believe that I was conducting all of this and they were actually singing it. In the process, we were giving voice to the *in-between* in a way that all of us could understand. It was great to be a part of this pilgrim chorus. It was like being in the often cacophonous choir of the Roman Catholic Church or another large and diverse community.

There's an often-used saying that there are two sides to every story. What that often means is that first there's "my side." Then there's "your side." And that's the whole story. There's nothing *in-between*. Whether we realized it or not, our pilgrim chorus was radically revising this perspective. It was letting us embody the fact that there are actually *three sides* to every story. There's an outside, an inside, and an animating Spirit moving *in-between*, uniting and transcending them both. And every single side of this story is personal. As I begin to experience my personal story in this three-dimensional way, I begin to see its three-fold character reflected in the bigger story that I share with everyone. I begin to experience the real importance of living in the *in-between* for the integrity of both my personal and our communal story.

No matter how hard I try I can't *sing* this *good news bad news in-between* trio all alone. I just can't do it. In order to sing it I have to have at least a couple of others join me, as I'm able to do in these retreats. Then we all get the chance to sing this impossible trio and to experience how it sounds when sung aloud. Although it's hard to reproduce, once you hear it, the sound of this cacophonous trio is awfully hard to forget.

Even though I can't sing it alone, what I can do alone is silently *live* the music of this trio. In its most radical sense, that's what I find living in the *in-between* to be really all about. It's about learning how to live a three-dimensional story as fully as I can, even if I'm the only one who can hear the music.

The dream of Ira taking me home by our journeying *in-between* the monastery and the university was one single dream. It was over when I woke up. The dream may be over but the *dreaming* lingers on within me like the melody of a long-forgotten song. More than thirty years later, I can still hear its silent music and the cacophony of our pilgrim chorus accompanying me on my journey of living creatively in the *in-between*.

14

The Strange Affair

Psalm 129
From my mother's womb
You have loved me into life,
and known my wonder.

—Soul Songs to God

There never has been a time in my life when I wasn't in love with God. There were many times when I wished I weren't in love with God. There were many times when I didn't act as though I was in love with God, and there were many times when I thought God couldn't care less about me. But there never was a time when I wasn't in love with God. We were engaged to be married right from the start, whenever that was.

Our love still hasn't been fully consummated, though. I'm leaving that up to God. As a result, at the very least, my courtship with my invisible Lover is now in its seventy-fifth year and counting. As courtships go, that makes for a pretty long engagement. It also makes for a very strange affair. What could a celibate misfit and an invisible Lover possibly see in one another?

But the way God makes love always has been a beacon for me. It's been a pillar of fire leading me through the darkest times in my life. It's as though, in the middle of the darkness, I would whisper, "Lord, to whom shall I go now?" Then I would wind up going wherever the wave of God's loving-kindness would carry me, even if it carried me further into the darkness. God's way of loving has also been a pillar of cloud leading me through the daylight times of my life.

By all customary standards, mine may be a long courtship and a very strange affair, but I wouldn't change it for the world. As I've experienced it, God's way of loving me is non-violent. It always honors my freedom. It's also benevolent, with no strings attached. It doesn't try to possess, or control, or change, or manipulate me. It simply wishes me well in the most empowering ways. It's an infinitely refreshing *Shalom*. It's also evocative and creative. Even when I'm at my worst, it calls forth the very best from so deep within me that it often isn't mine at all—and I know it.

I hesitate to say this, but it's true. I find God's way of loving to be more than simply divine. I find it to be absolutely divinizing. It's as though, while I'm worshipping God, God is worshipping God in me. It feels like the one God worshipping God. That's why I hesitate to say it. This strange affair is strange enough but this makes this strange affair sound stranger still, even to me. But that doesn't make it any less true.

I believe that, deep down, it was this way of loving that led me to want to live celibately from the time I learned that there was another option. Even as a teenager, I knew deep down that I wasn't being called to express my loving genitally with one person. I was being called to love everyone just as God loves them. I could also see that "playing the field," as some of my buddies were doing regardless of the personal fallout that came with it, just wasn't an option for me.

Most basically, it was also God's way of loving that led me to become a Norbertine priest. I experienced these priests loving us just as Jesus did, by breaking bread and helping others in a prayerful, self-effacing way. They made God's way of loving visible and tangible for me. I didn't become celibate in order to be a priest, as many of my fellow priests did. I became a priest as part of being celibate.

It was also God's way of loving that got me back on track every time I felt that I had completely lost my way or that I couldn't possibly go on.

I didn't know it at the time but when I returned to Daylesford Abbey in Pennsylvania after teaching in Chicago for four years, my strange affair with God was about to take a very significant next step. I didn't know what I'd wind up doing when I got back to the Abbey, but it felt good to be walking barefoot again with brothers and sisters whom I knew and loved in a place that had become sacred for me. It was good to be home again.

I soon was assigned to give retreats and Intensive Journal workshops in our newly founded Institute for Religion and Culture; to be available for individual spiritual direction; to care for the Abbey grounds; to serve on the Abbot's Council; and to move to the former caretaker's house at the edge of the property where, as Vocation Director, I could welcome those who were considering joining our way of life. If I could squeeze in a little writing on the side, that'd be good, too. It was a perfect fit for what I felt I was being called to at the time, especially the more simple and solitary setting of the caretaker's house.

Before long I found myself renovating the former caretaker's house so that it could serve as a small house of prayer and retreat for those seeking solitude and silence just as I was. I named the place Emmaus in honor of the two disciples in Luke's Gospel whose disenchantment was turned into deep enchantment and elated witness after meeting the Risen Christ on the road to Emmaus.

As I got more involved in the work of rebuilding and landscaping, I felt that what I was being led to do now that I had left the classroom was to take my theology out of my head and put it in my hands and heart so that eventually the environment itself would be the guru for me and perhaps also for our retreatants and guests. So I went about learning how to do some carpentry, gardening, tree planting and care, retrofitting, roofing, housekeeping, interior decorating, and even a little cooking on the side. In the process, the environment began to reward me for the attention I was giving it by beginning to be my spiritual teacher.

As I went about this work I began to feel that I was not only creating symbols but that I was actually learning to live symbolically. That was a thrill. It was as though I was being led by a river of symbols bubbling up from deep within me. In a sense, these symbols were mine but, at the same time, they were much more than mine. This made me feel as though a Mystery was unfolding within and around me and making me part of it. I had never experienced this before as intensely as I began to experience it now. It made me very attentive to the present moment and very mindful of the quality of what I was doing. Whatever I was doing, I was to do it whole-heartedly or not at all. I was very aware that I was living on sacred ground.

In a retreat that I was leading I once tried to sum up the journey that was underlying this experience by sententiously saying, "The longest journey in the world is the journey from our head to our heart."

A woman chimed right in by calling out, "Yes. And the journey from our heart to our head is equally long!" *Touché*.

In this simple exchange, we had succeeded in piecing together the "two sides plus one" of the story as I've experienced it. Or, better yet, we succeeded in piecing together the two sides of the cycle of living meditatively by moving from head-to-heart and heart-to-head again and again so that our hands can begin to give a thoughtful labor of love to the world.

I was doing a lot of different things at the time but I began to realize that, underneath them all, the work that united them all was the work of building a place where I could live with my Love. This was my labor of love. I was building a love nest. That became more apparent to me when I discovered a spring house on the property that wanted to be a chapel. It became even more obvious shortly after that when I uncovered an abandoned pool house at the edge of the Abbey grounds that wanted to be a hermitage where I could live apart from my ministry and community. So I renovated them both under the expert direction of two carpenters who were out of work and, with the Abbot's personal blessing, moved into the hermitage. I called the renovated spring house "The Chapel of the Baptist" in memory of the ancient hermit chapel in Prémontré, France, where our community was founded in 1120. I called the hermitage "Siloam," thinking of Thomas Merton's troubled search for solitude, and the waters through which Jesus gave sight to the man born blind. As I remember this time, I still consider it to have been one of the most creative times in my life.

Underlying all of the work I was doing at this time was a project that came to me after re-reading Mahatma Gandhi's book, *My Experiment with Truth*. I was even more deeply moved by reading this book at this time than when I first read it as a young college student. The question it left me with was, "What is *my* experiment with?"

My immediate answer to this question was, "Loving. My

experiment is with loving." So I went about organizing and intensifying "my experiment with loving" by adopting some spiritual exercises that might foster it, meditating on the Canticle of Canticles, and by asking God to teach me how to love.

I didn't know what I was asking for. I no sooner started asking God to teach me how to love than love began coming at me from every side. I stopped designing exercises. They weren't necessary. I had more loving than I could handle. So I started asking God, with a certain urgency, to teach me how to handle lovingly the surprising form "my experiment with loving" was taking.

Then one night I heard a voice say, "Francis, you've got it all wrong."

"I do?" I asked.

"Yes, you do," the voice replied. "*You're* not conducting this experiment. You *are* the experiment. I'm conducting you."

This radically reversed my customary point of view. It made all the difference in the world for me, too. It wasn't limited to loving, either. It applied to all that I am and all that I'm doing. God is conducting the experiment in loving that I am. It was hard to wrap my managerial, strategic-planning mind around that. In fact, it was impossible. I just had to learn to live with it. As I did, it surely took a big burden off me.

Shortly after that, as a young woman was leaving the parlor after a touchingly intimate session in spiritual direction, I heard someone telling me a love story. It was as though it was being dictated to me and I was to write it down right away. The story was called, "The Strange Affair."

> *A woman once went to see her Rabbi. "Rabbi," she said, "I'm in love with you!"*
>
> *The Rabbi looked at her with compassion. "Woman," he replied, "you're in love with yourself." He said nothing more.*
>
> *The woman went away brokenhearted. She felt that she had been rejected.*

Much later, the woman returned. "Rabbi," she said, "it's true! I'm in love with my self! Deep down, I'm a beautiful, wonderful woman!"

The Rabbi looked at her with compassion. "Woman," he replied, "you're in love with the whole world." He said nothing more.

The woman went away puzzled. "He must be crazy," she thought. "How can I be in love with the whole world?"

After a long time, the woman returned. "Rabbi," she said, "it's true! I'm in love with the whole world! I love to watch the sun rise. I love the rain, and the moon, and the stars, and the birds, and all the marvelous plants and animals that surround us. I love my little cottage and this grand old village. It's true, Rabbi. I'm in love with the whole world!"

The Rabbi looked at her with compassion. "Woman," he said, "you're in love with your God." He said nothing more.

The woman went away deeply perplexed. "I'm in love with my God?" she thought. "What could that possibly mean?"

Years later, the woman returned. "Rabbi," she said, "it's true! I'm in love with my God. I love God with all my heart, and with all my soul, and with all my strength. Rabbi, I'm in love with my God."

The Rabbi looked at her with compassion. "Woman," he said, "you love me."

The woman was furious. "Didn't you hear what I said?" she shouted. "I'm in love with my God! Who do you think you are?"

She stormed out of the Rabbi's house, slamming the door behind her.

After a long time, the woman returned. "Rabbi," she said, "I love you."

"Well, so be it!" the Rabbi exclaimed, and the two of them embraced like long-lost friends.

Then they stepped back and looked at one another with a compassion their faces could hardly contain.

"My dear friend," the Rabbi whispered, "we love enemies and strangers."

The woman nodded, and left without saying a word.

As time went by, all kinds of people began coming to the woman with their troubles. They would open their hearts to her and ask her advice. Even her own people began to call her "Rabbi."

One day a young man came to see her. "Rabbi," he said, "I'm in love with you!"

The woman looked at him with compassion. "Young man," she replied, "you're in love with yourself." She said nothing more... She said nothing more.

One evening, when we were having dinner together, Ira and I started telling stories, as we sometimes would. When I told him the story of "The Strange Affair," he broke out laughing. "Full cycle!" he said. "It goes full cycle!" Then he paused for a moment, smiled at me, and whispered, "And that came to you right off the top of your head, didn't it?"

"Yep," I smiled, "right off the top of my head."

Of course, as we both knew, this story didn't come to me right off the top of my head. It came to me right from the bottom of my heart. It came right from the heart of "my experiment with loving." Without giving all the details, "The Strange Affair" sums up all that I was learning in my experiment with loving. In a way, it's the whole story.

When I meditatively put my life in one hand and "The Strange Affair" in the other, I found they were mirror images. Meditating in the empty space in-between, I was first impressed by the courage of the woman to declare her love so openly. That courage couldn't have come to her all at once. It must have built up over time. She must have been carrying this love around within her heart for quite a while until she just couldn't keep it secret anymore.

I was then impressed by her docility. She took some very heavy hits from the Rabbi at some very vulnerable times but, after re-grouping, her love just kept growing and getting deeper and deeper.

My meditation then began to focus on the silence in-between

the words of the Rabbi and the woman. It was there in the silent blank spaces, above all, that I experienced the mysterious transforming action of love taking place. It was happening right there, in the silent emptiness in-between the words.

Then I began to be struck by how many forms the woman's love had taken along the way. It just kept deepening and expanding. It embraced the Rabbi, her Self, the world, her God, her friends, enemies and strangers, and a love-sick young man. For her, love was a many-splendored experience. It was the fruit of a very long journey—a very long "experiment"—in loving.

My meditative attention then turned to the Rabbi, to his apparent insensitivity to the woman's declaration of love, and to how deeply his curt response must have wounded her. "He said nothing more." How brutal can you get in the face of a loving woman's pain?

But then I recalled the apparent insensitivity of another Rabbi when a woman begged him to heal her daughter. Jesus wouldn't even talk to her. He just let her overhear him saying to his disciples, "I was sent only to the lost sheep of the house of Israel." When the woman kept asking for his help, his only reply was, "It is not right to take the food of the children and throw it to the dogs."

The woman responded, "Please, Lord, for even the dogs eat the scraps that fall from the table of their masters."

The only thing the Rabbi could say to that was, "O, woman, great is your faith! Let it be done for you as you wish." And her daughter was healed. What a reluctant Rabbi. And what a passionately loving woman.

Then I began thinking that perhaps the Rabbi in "The Strange Affair" was a reluctant teacher too. Maybe he was testing this woman with his "tough love" to see whether she was a tourist in love, or a pilgrim in loving. When it became clear that she was a pilgrim, they embraced as kindred spirits.

Then I began to admire how deeply the Rabbi must have loved this woman and how disciplined he was in the art of loving. He could easily have made this a very short, and a very familiar, story by responding to the woman's initial declaration of love by going to bed with her. But he didn't. That made all the difference. It let the long, painstaking journey into loving go full cycle.

Then I began to realize that the Rabbi certainly must have made this journey again and again himself. Otherwise, how could he have been so familiar with the loving steps the woman was being called to take? Realizing this, I began to see the Rabbi in a very different light. I began to see him, not as a glacial stoic but as a tremendous lover.

Then I found myself in the woman's heart again as she began to realize that, all along, the Rabbi was loving her just as God was loving her. I felt that must have been the ordaining moment for her. It must have been the moment that empowered her to begin loving the Rabbi and others in the very same non-possessive way that God was loving her through the Rabbi.

I was deeply touched when the woman's own People began calling her "Rabbi." For thousands of years, that title has been reserved for men only. Now, here she is, being recognized as "Rabbi" by her own People.

She had earned it by being faithful to a long, heart-wrenching Exodus into loving, just as her People had been. I was deeply moved by this thought. It made me wonder whether the young man would be gifted with a similar courage and fidelity so that God's way of loving would continue being passed on through him, or whether the story of "The Strange Affair" would end right there, at least for him.

In any event, "The Strange Affair" doesn't end right there for me. It keeps telling me the whole story of my "experiment in loving" in ever-changing ways. This is a story I'm not meant merely to tell. It's a story I'm called to live. It's my story.

As I live through "The Strange Affair," I won't just be courting God. I'll be imitating the loving woman by courting other persons, my true Self, the world, my God, friends, strangers, enemies, and all kinds of people, including love-sick young and not-so-young ones. What's more, I'll be courting them all at the same time. This means that my experiment in loving will be a longer courtship than I had originally planned—or could ever imagine. It also means that my experiment in loving will never stop being a very "Strange Affair."

15

Getting it All Together

Now that I have it all together, I forget where I put it.
  —An anonymous bumper sticker

$\mathcal{A}$ strange thing happened to me on the way to getting it all together. It kept falling apart. This was a real problem. Getting it all together wasn't just an option for me. It was a solemn obligation that came at me from every direction.

My parents wanted me to get it all together from day one. After the mess I made of day one, they changed their minds. They wanted me to get it all together from day two. Right away, I was off to a very shaky start.

The Sisters who taught me in grade school had a thousand ways of making it clear that they wanted me to get it all together *right now*, or else. Of course that made it kind of fun for me to let it all fall apart. But then there'd be hell for me to pay for not getting it all together. And I was only six years old!

The Church really wanted me to get it all together, too. It still does. Getting it all together began to feel to me like the Church's price of admission. This didn't bother me all that much at first. But when I got into adolescence, this pressure to get it all together really began to bother me. It didn't just bother me on the outside, either. It bothered me on the inside. My own conscience began pushing me to get it all together *right now* or else go to hell. For me, this is the worst kind of being bothered.

Of course, I had a fallback position for that. I could always go to confession. And that's just what I was doing, too. I was *always* going to confession. The priests must have seen me coming, and thought to themselves, "I can't believe it. Here he comes again! Francis the Confessor."

But, if they did think that, they were very good at keeping it to themselves, since they always welcomed me as though they had never seen me before, and kept assuring me that God thought that I really had it all together.

I think that part of the problem at the time was that I was taking Jesus' words literally when he said, "You are to be perfect as your heavenly Father is perfect." No matter who you are, having it as all together as God does is asking an awful lot. Our All-American culture only compounds this.

But, thank goodness, as teenagers we finally did get it all together. At least we thought we did. This put a lot of pressure on those of us who knew deep down inside that this wasn't really true, which meant that we would just have to learn how to *look like* we had it all together. I can't speak for the others, but I know, in my case, that was a sorry sight. I never was much of an actor. Either I didn't have an act or I couldn't figure out what my act should be. At any rate, going around acting as though I had my act all together began to feel pretty stupid to me. Deep down, I began to wonder if I could find a community somewhere in which I wouldn't have to pretend that I had it all together.

If I thought the Norbertines was that community, I was dead wrong. At that time you had to have it all together or else you'd get sent home right away. I wonder where we found so many young men who had achieved such admirable integration so early in life. At any rate, I knew that I wasn't one of them. I know that because of the sleepless night I spent before I took my lifetime vows. Somehow or other I knew for sure that the community would refuse to accept my vows in the morning and would send me home. I also knew that they would be dead wrong in doing that because I had no doubt at all that God was calling me to be one of them whether I had it all together or not. The fact that the Master of Professed laughed at me when I told him about my misgivings didn't change my fears at all. I still spent a sleepless night.

But, in the morning, I made my solemn vows in the hands of the Abbot. I guess the community thought I finally had it all together.

If I really wanted to slip under the "having it all together" radar, being ordained a priest in 1960 was definitely not the way to do it.

At that time, most Catholics had the priest squarely on their radar as an *alter Christus*, "another Christ." It was hard to have it any more all together than that. In Ireland, the policemen would even stop traffic so that the priest could safely walk across the street. I know that because they stopped traffic for me, and I was only a seminarian.

I think that part of my great attraction to doing strategic planning was that I assumed that it was a failsafe way of getting it all together. Once we were able fully to articulate and implement our strategic plan, we would have it all together. It was as simple as that. So was I in thinking so.

On the other hand, I found it increasingly hard for me to have it all together when I began to realize that I was living with a restless heart; walking barefoot through so many transitions; changing my name every time I turned around; living as a stranger in a strange land; feeling like a misfit; spending most of my time in the *in-between*; and being caught up in a life-long "strange affair" with God and company. This made living somewhere *in-between* having it all together and not having it all together a way of life for me.

To take some of the pressure off myself I developed an "indefinite postponement strategy." I began to think that I might have it all together in some other life but, for the "time being," I'd just have to keep doing the best that I could. Of course, as the song reminded me, "tomorrow never comes."

As helpful as it was, I can now see that my I.P.S. strategy was just a temporary adjustment. For me, the real shift came when I finally began to trust the data of my own inner experience and to question the personal and communal assumptions, expectations, and dogmas that were covering over my own experience. That's when I began not merely studying and teaching about rites of passage in creative persons' lives, but also honoring these rites in my own life. That's also when I began relating to my life as an ongoing process and not as some predetermined product that I had to piece together as diligently as I could. This shift in how I envisioned and related to my life made a tremendous difference in how I personally approached "getting it all together."

Appropriately enough, the gift that symbolized this difference for me came, not in a personal dream, but in a brightly-colored, eye-grabbing, All-American advertisement. One day, as I hurried through the Chicago airport on my way to giving an Intensive Journal Workshop, an attractive back-lighted advertisement caught my eye. It was an advertisement about ten feet high and fifteen feet long, give or take an inch or two, with a picture on it of the biggest jigsaw puzzle I've ever seen. At the bottom of the picture was a boldly printed message: "GET IT ALL TOGETHER." Then I noticed that, from the side, the missing piece of the jigsaw puzzle was quietly being added. The understated message that accompanied it read, "*Buy Newsweek.*"

"That's it!" I thought. "I've been treating my life as though it's a jigsaw puzzle that I have to put together all by myself. But, deep down, I know that's not the case. My life's really a deeply moving journey that only I can make. It's not just a product or a thing. It's an ongoing process. It's the animating movement of 'I am' unfolding through time. Think of that."

I realize that this isn't exactly what the advertisement was designed to tell me. In fact, it was designed to tell me just the opposite. But I was grateful anyway for what it said so graphically to me.

This simple shift in image from jigsaw puzzle to journey let me experience my whole life as an ongoing yeah-boo-wow story. On the one hand, from time to time, "having it all together"—"Yeah!" On the other hand, from time to time, "everything falling apart"—"Boo!" And in-between, the most mysterious journey of my life moving through them both—"Wow!"

And that wasn't all. After a while I began to see that this shift in basic image from jigsaw puzzle to journey completely changed what "having it all together" meant to me. A woman at an Intensive Journal workshop that I was leading helped me begin to realize this. As I began the workshop, she contentiously asked, "And how about the guy who designed this journal, does he have his life all together?" I recognized this right away as a very loaded "have it all together question." It was like the biblical put down, "Doctor, cure yourself." In not too veiled a way it was saying, "If he doesn't have it all together himself, he doesn't have anything to say to me." A great way to avoid *doing* the inner work.

Without even thinking about it I replied, "The man who created this journal is a good friend of mine. I know from being with him personally that, at times, he has it all together. At other times, it's all falling apart. He seems to know the difference, though, and how to move with whatever is happening in his life. That strikes me as a very helpful skill that we may be able to develop by working in this journal."

I don't know whether or not this reply satisfied the woman since she never told me. But I do know that it changed what "having it all together" means to me. For me, "having it all together" began to mean knowing where I am at the present moment in my journey and being faithful to it every step of the way, even when everything's falling apart. So, I *always* have it together if I know where I am in the movement of my life and what's happening *here and now*. This really boggles my mind, but it deeply consoles my spirit. It gives me a whole other take on the "walking barefoot through the desert" times in my journey. It means that if it's time for walking barefoot and that's what I'm doing, I have it all together, even if it's all falling apart. Of course, this doesn't make much sense to my jigsaw-puzzle-piecing-together self, but it makes eminently good sense to the restless-hearted pilgrim within me. It means that if I'm a misfit and I know it, I have it all together. It lets me see that, when Jesus cries out on the cross, "My God, my God, why have you forsaken me?" he has it all together. This boggles my mind, but it delights my restless heart.

This very different experience of "having it all together" made me even more attentive to how my life was unfolding and more diligent in exploring it through meditation, study, writing, and spiritual teaching. Eventually, I was also heartened to see how helpful my emphasis on attending to our own *LifeProcess* was for those whom I taught in retreats, workshops, and spiritual direction, and how much sense it made to them in light of their own experience. In the process, I began to realize that, in many different ways, this focus on the dynamics, discipline, and recurrent forms of the spiritual journey had been the center of my spiritual concern and teaching for a very long time. It was the unifying lifework underlying many, if not all, of the other works I had been doing. So, in 1992, I expressed this symbolically by founding *The Center for Process Spirituality*. A priest I knew who suspected that there might be something terribly unorthodox, if not heretical, going on under my new umbrella of "Process Spirituality" once asked me at lunch, "Fran, can you tell me in one word what Process Spirituality is all about?"

"Sure, John," I replied, "it's all about process."

"Oh," he said, and went back to eating his lunch.

In an effort to invite him to enlarge on his concern a bit I added, "If you want to know what it's all about in *two* words, John, it's all about Process Spirituality."

After about a decade or so I began to think that "Process Spirituality" might not actually be the best name for my lifework or for the Center. I got an early intimation of this when Ira Progoff reacted to it by saying, "'Process Spirituality' is going to be a problem." Later on I saw how, in many circles, "process" was being quite narrowly equated with the teachings of a specific modern philosopher. At the same time, product-oriented "spiritualities" were multiplying not just like rabbits but like religious jigsaw puzzles and threatening a more organic and unitive view of the spiritual journey. What I was working with could be enriched by both of these developments but I didn't want it to be equated with either of them. I also didn't want to be obliged to start lecturing on how what I was doing differed from both of them. That would have taken my lifework back up into my head which was exactly what I was being called to avoid. So, as I often did with my own name, I changed the name of the Center to "The Center for *LifeProcess* Awareness." For me, that really said what I felt my life and my lifework are all about. They're all about being very attentive to how my life is unfolding.

A few years later a woman approached me during a retreat in meditative writing that I was leading at our Priory in New Mexico. "I've been looking all around here for the Center for *LifeProcess* Awareness," she said, "and I can't find it. You know what I'm thinking now?"

"No," I said. "What are you thinking?"

"I'm thinking that *you're* the Center for *LifeProcess* Awareness. You are, aren't you?"

"Yes," I replied. "I'm the Center for LifeProcess Awareness. And so are *you*."

I don't know whether this made much sense to her at the time, but it's really true. If she had continued the conversation by asking, "Fran, can you tell me in one word what being a Center for *LifeProcess* Awareness is all about?" I would have replied, "Sure, Jane, if you really want to know, it's all about loving."

If she had said "Oh," and had gone out to lunch, I would have tagged along and added, "If you really want to know what it's all about in *two* words, Jane, it's all about loving God."

Even though I think that would have described the process in *LifeProcess* quite well as I experience it, it probably wouldn't have made much more sense to the retreatant than the classic "becoming One with the Triune God" response does to most people. She was just beginning to take the spiritual journey seriously, and it usually takes quite a while to realize that it's actually all about becoming one with Love. At least it took me quite a while to learn it and to realize that that's what's really going on. But, in its own good time, that's where being a center of *LifeProcess* awareness gradually led me.

16

Rebuilding the Church

*We'll know we have been raised from the dead
when everything becomes a door—*

*...when every single thing....
...becomes a door....*

—Last Night I Died

*U*sually when I have the sense the Lord is closing a door on me there really isn't much question about it. If it doesn't slam in my face, it slams loudly shut behind me. Even though that often hurts, I've learned to be thankful for it. I've also learned that trying to put my foot in the door at this time is a good way to get it broken, especially since I'm often already going barefoot by this time. The previous two years had been banner years for doors closing in my life and often on my foot. To be exact, four very big doors closed on me, one right after the other.

After I had worked myself practically to exhaustion for eight years at Daylesford Abbey, the Abbot gave me a year off to rebuild my strength, to put things in perspective, and to discern whether or not I was being called to a more contemplative way of living than our apostolically-oriented community can usually support.

I was very grateful that this time, the Abbey door closed more gently on me than most doors previously had. For a year or so before it actually happened, I had been meditatively anticipating the door closing by walking with the mantra, "The ending of a season....the ending of a season...."

That mantra said it all for me, not in detail of course, but in essence. I could not only feel the change of season in the air, I could already smell the burning leaves. No muss. No fuss. Just a little nostalgic tug at my heart while I was facing what seemed already to be a matter of fact. It would have been nice, of course, had that most creative summer continued, but it was clearly over now. Fall and winter were on the way. I could already hear the door gently closing behind me.

During the year of discernment that I spent living with the Camaldolese Hermits in Big Sur, California, it became clear to me that, while I was greatly enriched by sharing their way of life, I was not being called to be a hermit of New Camaldoli. I was being called to continue to try to discover how to live as a contemplative priest of Prémontré. I knew from painful experience that this would be much more challenging and much more creative for me than simply moving into a well-established, existing hermitage. Bam! went the hermit door behind me. The strange thing was that I knew right away that the door opening in front of me would be a hermit door as well. I just couldn't see how in the world that could happen.

So I decided to return to my Abbey in Philadelphia both as the next step in my journey of discernment and as a gesture of sincere good will to the new Abbot. Fortunately, when he received my application, the confrere who chaired the personnel committee there thoughtfully called to tell me that I must be crazy. He said that I was a *persona non grata* at the Abbey.

It isn't a very nice thing to be a *persona non grata* in our community. It's something like being a misfit in the popularly unpopular sense of that word. So I thanked my brother profusely for sparing all of us that kind of grief at a time when we all had more than enough grief than we could handle. Bam! went the Abbey door—again! Actually, this time I felt greatly relieved to hear it close before I got too close to it.

By a real stroke of Providence, I was able to spend the following year living in what I called my "tree house hermitage" of Saint Clare at Presentation Center, a beautiful retreat center high in the Santa Cruz Mountains in California. I served as the resident chaplain and retreat master there. My hermitage was perched on the edge of a redwood canyon. The trees came up from below to embrace it. I slept out on a screened-in porch that let me be part of the beautiful watches of the night. The last time I had been with Saint Clare was when she welcomed me to Assisi for my diaconate retreat. Our getting together again in California made this a very special year.

At the end of the year, however, the Sisters there decided that their long-term interests would be better served if they replaced me with a priest of the local diocese. Even though I didn't appreciate the decision very much, I could appreciate the logic of it. Bam! went the retreat house and hermitage doors behind me.

While all of these closing doors were painful and confusing in their own way, the nice thing about them for me was that they were all "graceful endings." With a lot of help from the Lord, it seemed that I was finally starting to get the hang of that part of the spiritual journey. As a psychologist friend closely watched me making my way through these two more or less peacefully unsettling years, she asked, "Fran, are *all* of your discernments as intense and protracted as this?" By that time there had been so many of them, I had to stop for a moment to think about it before saying, "I'm afraid so." I guess I'm just an intense sort of guy who needs to look at all the options.

But I've also learned that the Lord doesn't close doors on me just because God likes slamming doors. As doors close like this they make me much more attentive to doors that I've been overlooking; doors that may still be open; closed doors that may be opening again; or doors that I may have to turn around one hundred and eighty degrees to see. I find this way of widening the scope of my attentiveness has a lot to do with my being able eventually to take a creative next step. As my scientist brother used to remind me, "Fran, if you only have an 'n' of one, you don't have a decision to make."

So I called my good friend Joel, the enthusiastic Prior of our new foundation in Albuquerque, New Mexico. I told him that I'd take it as a sign that I was meant to come to New Mexico if a position as a spiritual director and teacher at a therapy center there that had been offered to me the previous year was still available. He said there was no chance of that being so, but that he'd call just to make sure.

That night he called me back in disbelief. The position was still open.

I still can't fully say how a door sounds when it opens as gently as this one did. There's an awesome silence about it. It makes me wonder. It makes me feel that I'm no longer alone and that I've just been given a very mysterious gift. This makes a deep joy and gratitude well up within me.

It's a gloriously sunny morning for driving into the Jemez Mountains. As I pass through the Pueblo of Walatowa and enter the Jemez Canyon that it guards, the deep, silent beauty of the canyon's red rock mesas welcomes me. It gives me the sense that I'm entering Sacred Ground. I enter very slowly and with prayerful reverence. I pray that this may be the place that God has prepared for me, the place where my long pilgrimage will finally come to an end. The farther I go into the canyon, the narrower, deeper, and more mysteriously beautiful it becomes. Finally, it opens out on the little village of Jemez Springs. I feel as though I've just passed through a magnificent open door.

Everything Becomes a Door

I'll know I've been raised from the dead
when everything becomes a door—
   every brick wall,
   every dead end,
   every Judas friend,
everything I see and smell and taste,
everything I think and feel and am,
every mountain top and valley bottom,
every birth and every death,
every joy and every pain,
every ecstasy and infidelity—
when every single thing
becomes a door
that opens to eternity
and I pass through

as I could never do
before.

Then I'll wonder why
I've spent so many years
just stopping at these doors;
why I've always pulled up short,
and turned arou nd,
and walked away,
instead of simply
passing through.
—Last Night I Died

Father Liam, the Provincial of the Servants of the Paraclete, opens my interview with him by saying, "Well, Fran, we'll do anything to have you join us here on staff. So tell me, what do we have to do for you to join us?"

I laugh and tell him that this is the most welcoming interview I've ever had in my life. The warm welcome continues as Father Liam invites me to join him and the staff at lunch, introduces me to some of the priests and brothers in the program, and shows me around the well-maintained facility. He ends the tour by opening the door of the basement laundry room for me, pointing to an isolated little cabin tucked into the trees down by the river, and saying with a knowing smile, "You may live there, if you'd like."

I must look as though I'm seeing a vision. The little cabin I'm staring at looks just like the hermitage I had dreamed about living in while I was with the hermits in Big Sur. Sometimes, when the Lord opens a door for me, he opens it very wide.

Then Liam and I work out the details.

When I get back to the Priory that night, one of my brothers asks me how the interview went.

"I was mesmerized by the canyon, Bob," I reply. "Those mountains are spiritually very charged."

"Well," he said, "the Indians say that God lives in those mountains. If that isn't it, maybe it's because ninety percent of the world's plutonium is buried in them."

Fortunately, the plutonium isn't buried in the canyon. It's buried on the other side of the mountain near the laboratories where the first atomic bomb was built.

I wasn't by any means the first pilgrim to find my way to Jemez Springs. I was the most recent in a very long line of pilgrims and penitents. About fifty years earlier, Father Fitzgerald had found his way into the canyon in search of a place to establish a new kind of monastery. Several doors had closed behind him earlier to give him that vision and to lead him here. A decisive door opened when he welcomed a homeless, penniless, man who was living on the street into his parish kitchen for a bite to eat. As they talked he discovered the man was an alcoholic priest who was living on the streets as a homeless person. After that meeting, Father Fitzgerald left his parish ministry convinced that we shouldn't be treating our priests that way. He then had to leave the religious community to which he belonged because helping troubled priests "wasn't their charism." So, with no support and very little money, he set out on a pilgrimage in search of the ruins of a church. Like Saint Francis of Assisi before him, he felt that the Lord was calling him to rebuild the Church. The way he hoped to do this was by helping alcoholic priests and brothers to change their ways—as the Gospel encourages us all to do—and to take the road to recovery by praying, fasting, and living with the Servants of the Paraclete for a while. In this way, he hoped to rebuild the Church one person at a time by helping to heal its spiritual leaders.

After making a long journey from place to place in search of a fitting site to undertake this work, Father Fitzgerald eventually found his way to the Archdiocese of Santa Fe. He felt that there the endless sunshine, the natural beauty, the distance from the demands of ministry, and the faith-filled tolerance that the Hispanic community showed for human frailty even in their priests, would provide a congenial atmosphere in which he could realize his vision. The bishop of Santa Fe welcomed him with open arms and took him on a long trip up into the mountains to see the isolated adobe ruins of the ancient church of Jemez Pueblo. There he discovered that the old motel just across the way was up for sale, together with a good parcel of land. Father Fitzgerald knew right away that this was where he would found his monastery. This is where he and the brothers and sisters who would join him would live, work, and pray with all their strength to rebuild the ruined Church one troubled priest and brother at a time. After such a long pilgrimage, he must have felt very grateful to see this door finally opening. He probably also suspected that there would be a very challenging and troubled future waiting for him and his little community on the other side of this door. And he was right.

Father Fitzgerald had already died by the time I came to Jemez Springs but the ancient ruins of the church of Jemez Pueblo still kept silent vigil there as an eloquent reminder of his original vision. Across the way, where the old motel had been, was an impressive new church and a state of the art therapeutic community for priests and brothers sharing the original Pueblo grounds and giving witness to Father Fitzgerald's dream still being realized by his followers. Knowing something of what his long journey must have been like, I felt it was a privilege to be invited to be part of this most creative and challenging ministry.

Like many religious at the time when he founded his therapeutic monastery, Father Fitzgerald didn't believe in psychology. He believed in the healing power of nature, the sacraments, the liturgy, three hours of meditative prayer a day, and a supportive community of faithful brothers and sisters. He hoped that the rest would take care of itself. Most of the devastating legal cases against the Servants of the Paraclete during the time I was on staff there stemmed from these early days.

A few years before I arrived, much of the original "open monastery" approach was changed. During that time, the program was completely redesigned to integrate the most modern therapeutic methods with the religious and spiritual core that was already firmly established there. The longer I was there, the more I experienced the result of this new approach to be a new kind of monastery. It was a monastery in which the inner work was being done by very talented men and women in a more conscious, sophisticated, intense, serious, and dedicated way than in any monastery where I had ever lived. Doing the inner work was not a matter of tradition, custom, ritual, or fashion for us here. It was a matter of utmost urgency. For the seven years I was there, I always felt it was a special blessing for me to be part of this dedicated community in such a Spirit-filled place at such a troubled time in the Church's life.

Part of the blessing of living here was that it allowed me to strike the creative balance I had been seeking for such a long time between solitary and communal living, and between contemplation and ministry. The weekly rhythm I was able to establish and, for the most part, maintain in my own life was one of going from three days of relatively intense solitude and prayer to four days of very demanding spiritual ministry. The more familiar I became with the destructive process at work within the lives of the priests and brothers who came here, the more clearly I could see that, in one form or another, this salutary rhythm was not just a personal preference or idiosyncrasy of mine. I saw it to be the underlying process through which the modern Church will be rebuilt, if it will be rebuilt at all. It convinced me that the Church will be rebuilt by persons, and especially by spiritual leaders, who embody this ongoing creative movement between praying and working, mystery and ministry, envisioning and realizing, suffering and serving, and being graced and being generous.

As I looked at our program I could see that this was the basic wisdom way to healthy and creative spiritual living that ran right through it, just as the Jemez River ran right through the Center's property. I saw that this was the underlying LifeProcess flowing through all that we as a staff and support community were doing and teaching. It was the animating rhythm that each of us in our own way was doing our best to embody, articulate, and help our guests internalize.

I began to realize that anyone who is really committed to following this wisdom way in a compulsive or addictive society, religious community, or Church, will probably wind up being an outcast. That seems to come with the turf. The lives of Jesus and all the prophets, together with the whole biblical tradition bear eloquent witness to this. Yet this rhythm of the wisdom way can be one of the most salutary ways to recognize the ruins from which the Church is to be rebuilt. Besides, as our work at Jemez Springs thoroughly documented for me, there are much worse ways of becoming an outcast than this.

I also realized that following this wisdom way means being willing to be in the world but not of it in certain extremely important ways. It may even mean being willing to be considered a mystic. Or perhaps, God help us, even a misfit. Why not? There's good precedent for that too.

All of which only deepened my conviction of how extremely urgent and potentially important for the Church our ministry in Jemez Springs actually was.

Among the other blessings that came to me through this ministry was that it helped me to understand, embrace, and embody my own sexuality in a way and at a depth that I had never done before. Prior to that, I had been thinking that, as a celibate, the less I knew about my sexuality the better. "Ignorance is bliss."

Ministering in the program made it clear to me that, unless my Guardian Angel was working overtime for me, ignorance of my own sexuality as a priest is not bliss. It's courting disaster. The meditative work that went with this realization greatly deepened my experience of what it meant really to believe in the Incarnation. It meant that I was being called to embody God in every aspect of my being, including in being sexual and all "that sort of thing." Of course, I had to keep this secret, except from myself, my spiritual director, and one of my therapist friends on staff with whom I would "reality check" from time to time. But it marked a major development in my on-going "experiment with loving."

This ministry also obliged me to revise, in a radical and much more realistic way, my understanding of the priesthood, the Church, religious life, prayer, and spirituality. This was a very heavy agenda. I wasn't just preparing a course on it, either. I was *taking* a course on it and making very attentive notes as I did.

Since much of the work we were doing at Jemez Springs was personal, communal, and spiritual shadow work, this ministry also made me look much more closely and much more honestly at my own shadow. I not only had to take off my combat boots, I had to look very closely at why I was wearing them in the first place. My combat boots weren't the only thing I had to take off and examine very closely, either. I had to enter shadow land and meditatively explore my whole wardrobe. My own shadow became my teacher in this work by confronting me with the darkness that was uniquely mine, and revealing the inner light that it cloaks and darkly reflects. For me, this meditative work was the most transformative part of my pilgrimage in Jemez Springs. It was what I seem to have been brought there for in the first place.

There were many, many deeply touching moments for me in my seven years in Jemez Springs. Some of the most memorable ones came while we were celebrating the Easter Vigil together. On that "most holy night," we would gather in the darkness to celebrate the Light shining from the face of the Risen Christ, while most of us were still going through the agony of a Friday that had not yet become even remotely Good. Together we would wholeheartedly sing "a new song" to the Risen Lord, while most of us were still standing at the tomb, wondering who would roll the stone away for us. For me, this was an experience of naked faith hidden in the pregnant darkness from which the Church was originally born and from which it will be rebuilt, if it will be rebuilt at all.

These touching Vigil moments were sometimes extended for me throughout the year when I would visit the church late at night before going to bed. I would just sit there for a while in the silent darkness gazing at the soft glow of the sanctuary lamp. Occasionally the timbers of the roof would creak like the hull of an old sailing ship out at sea. Otherwise, the church was completely silent. I was sitting alone in the Presence. Then, from within the silence, I would hear a priest begin to cry. We would sit there, alone and yet together, praying through our tears in the dark.

I will never forget those touching moments taking place in the darkness at the heart of the Church. I will never forget them.

Ira Progoff liked to say that a meaningful work is one that you would do for nothing, but it's nice if you get paid for it too. For me, the life and ministry I did in Jemez Springs was a most meaningful work. If I could have, I would willingly have paid the Servants for the privilege of doing it. Of course, I never told them that.

As a theologian who had been studying psychology rather intensely for a while, one of the things I was really looking forward to in coming to Jemez Springs was being able to work out and articulate an integrating approach to psychology and spirituality. At first, I was a bit disappointed that this wasn't happening. It took a while before I began to realize that it *was* happening, but not in the intellectual, academic way I had expected. It was actually happening in between us. Right in the middle of our mutual respect, collaborative ministry, and creative interaction, psychology, spirituality, physiology, and ministry were being fully integrated. We didn't have the time or inclination as a staff to articulate fully *how* this was happening, but most of us knew full well that it was.

Most of us also knew that something else was happening between us that none of us could take credit for. We all simply went about faithfully working hard, giving our presentations, suggesting important readings, meeting with bishops and superiors, writing our reports, conferring together as a team, counseling, supporting and challenging our guests, and joining them in prayer and at table. But, when one of our guests would finally "bottom out," see the light, and begin to turn around in earnest, we could only celebrate it. We knew that we didn't make it happen. It wasn't our doing. All we could do was marvel at it and rejoice.

For me, this was the greatest blessing of all. It was as though one of our guests had been baptized by fire, or had been ordained a second time, and now had begun to see spiritually why he had been ordained in the first place.

When I had the chance, I would ask a guest who was leaving the program what had been the most important experience for him in his time at Jemez Springs. The answer often surprised and delighted me.

One priest told me, "Discovering and embracing my shadow. If I had known and accepted that I had a shadow, I never would have had to come here." I think he and I were kindred spirits.

A young Vietnamese priest answered my question by saying, "Most important thing? Most important thing. Most important thing....for me....is change of direction I go in. When I come here, I go to misery. When I leave, I go to happiness! That's most important thing." And his face lit up like a candle.

In the end, facilitating this radical kind of conversion, this radical change of the direction in which a priest's or brother's life is heading, is what our own life and ministry as the staff in Jemez Springs was all about. When we saw a conversion like this happening, we were witnessing a mystery and a miracle unfolding before our eyes. We were witnessing the Church being rebuilt in one of her spiritual leaders. For us, this was the really Good News.

The newspapers weren't at all interested in reporting this kind of news, however. They were much too busy reporting the scandalously bad news that had brought some of our guests to Jemez Springs and that was bringing the Church to its knees and to the brink of financial and spiritual bankruptcy. But to us, this Good News of radical conversion was the news that really mattered. It kept us going in an extremely demanding ministry. Being a part of this God-given good news was our modest contribution to the ongoing conversion of the Church. It also kept us mindful of the great importance of what we were doing and of the courage of Father Fitzgerald's original vision of rebuilding the Church from the ruins up, one person at a time.

We'll know we have been raised from the dead
when everything becomes a door—....

...when every single thing....
...becomes a door....

17

In the Shadow of Mother Church

In the shadow of your wings, I shout for joy.

—Psalm 63: 8

Beware of the one who casts no shadow.

—A Chinese Proverb

*E*ven though we had a big, beautiful church at Daylesford Abbey, the little Chapel of the Baptist that I had rebuilt there from the ruins of our old spring house was still one of my favorite places to pray.

In one way, it wasn't far at all from Emmaus, the house of prayer that I had established on the edge of the Abbey grounds. I could see it from the kitchen window. But, in another way, it felt like it was centuries away from there. For me, walking down to the Chapel felt like going all the way back into the hermit caves of Francis at Assisi or Benedict at Subiaco, or the catacombs of the early Christians, or the cave at Bethlehem. Especially the cave at Bethlehem.

The Chapel of the Baptist was partially sunken into the ground so that the water from an underground spring could fill the ditch that lined its walls before flowing through the foundation to fill the pond outside. I had to go down five stone steps in order to enter it. As may have been customary in spring houses, the lintel of the doorway was quite low. To get in, I had to bend over a bit so as not to bump my head. These rituals always felt to me like acts of threshold reverence. So did getting myself all cut up by the thorns of the wild rose bushes that completely covered the doorway with white roses when I first came across the spring house ruins and tried to enter them. That was the unforgettable beginning of it being a very special place for me.

Once inside, the interior might come to some as a surprise. The walls were not the carefully finished and mortared field stone of the outside that gave it the look of an early colonial building. They were rough rocks randomly stacked up on one another that were held together with ordinary mud. This gave the interior the feel of an ancient cave. At the far end of the small, damp space was a very large rock with the Word of God lying open on it. The rock was so big that I had to take down part of the doorway wall to get it into the Chapel. From under the rock, water welled up from the underground spring and flowed in every direction. A large, rough-hewn wooden cross with a Star of David carved right through the center of it hung from the ceiling. At night, the soft light from a sanctuary lamp that I had attached to the back of the cross flickered through the Star of David and cast moving shadows on a small portion of the stone wall behind it. Being here felt like being in a very ancient place of prayer, especially at night when I would sit in the darkness listening to the flowing water. Then I'd pray that everything I'd say and do would flow from the underground spring just as freely as the water did from beneath this Chapel.

One morning as Lent began, I went down to the Chapel to pray. As I arrived I saw a Canada goose sitting there quietly on the ground right next to the pond. She had made her nest and was beginning to sit on her eggs. When she saw me, she let me know right away that she preferred to be alone. So I honored that but I brought her some bread every day anyway. She seemed to be grateful, too, since by evening the bread would be gone. Gradually, she'd even let me come a little closer to offer her the bread so that she wouldn't have to get off her nest to eat it.

When I went down to the Chapel on Easter morning, it was as though she was waiting to show me something. There she was, standing as proud as could be over her new-born chick in the bright sun of Easter morning, protecting the smallest gosling I've ever seen in her shadow. What an Easter present!

"In the shadow of your wings, I shout for joy."

Like almost everyone else in our South Philadelphia neighborhood, I grew up in the shadow of the Catholic Church. In fact, I grew up in the shadow of a trinity of Catholic churches, all within easy walking distance of each other. Ours was still basically a neighborhood of second or third generation immigrants, and its boundaries were marked by King of Peace, "the Italian church," Saint Aloysius, "the German church," and Saint Gabriel, "the Irish church." We had to be very clear about which church we "belonged to," but after that, there was a lively ecumenical movement going on from church to church. After all, we were all Catholics.

It wasn't a doctrinal ecumenical movement, though. It was actually one of religious convenience and social enrichment. Each parish was still the center of an ethnic community's whole religious and social life, with the priests and sisters serving pretty much as coordinators of it all. It was like an extended family. That gave the wider community a rich diversity of Masses, schools, prayer styles, ethnic celebrations, picnics, devotions, dances, "block parties," bingo games, processions, feast days, boy and girl scout troops, sports teams, clubs, pious associations, service projects, raffles, and even priests and sisters, to mix and match and choose from. Without any effort, we could have produced the classic movie "Going My Way" in four languages! At the time, we had no private phones in our homes. Television was at least a decade away from appearing and when it did it was available at first only in the bars, and then only for a few hours a day. So this ecumenical movement was pretty much the only show in town. It was the center of our lives.

As strange as it may seem to young people today, this was the "Mother Church" in whose warm, nurturing shadow I grew up. For me, the Church wasn't an "it." It wasn't some remote mega-institution. The Church was a living "We"—a greatly extended family whose center was right there in the heart of our own neighborhood. When, much later, the Second Vatican Council declared that, first and foremost, we were "the People of God," I was pleased to hear it, but it didn't surprise me at all. What else could we be and be as alive and well and faithful and courageous as we actually were in our neighborhood?

That meant that the warm, nurturing shadow in which I grew up wasn't coming from outer space somewhere. It was coming from all of us. It was coming from our faithful mothers, fathers, sisters, brothers, relatives, next-door neighbors, sisters, and priests. We didn't put it this way, but this was the shadow in which we lived and moved and had our being, and grew in wisdom, age, and grace, before God and each other, if we grew at all. The shadow of "Mother Church" was *our* shadow.

It seems rather stupid to me now to ask myself if there was another side to this shadow in which we all grew up, a side other than its warm, nurturing, benevolent one. Of course there was. There was a dark, malevolent, destructive, controlling side of this shadow as well. You could hardly miss it. It was all over the place, including within each of us. We didn't talk much about it, though. In fact, we did all that we could to keep it a personal, or a family, or a parish, or a neighborhood secret. We got very good at that, too. After all, we were "the People of God," so we had to look good. But People of God or not, we all seemed to know that this malevolent shadow was there and that we were casting it. Angels probably don't have this problem but, none of us, including our sisters and priests, were angels. We were just Roman Catholics.

I wasn't going to confession every other day because I was walking in the light. My priests never talked to anybody about it of course, but I was going to confession so frequently because I was starting to cast a dark shadow myself. I knew that I wasn't the only one who needed to go to confession too, but for the most part, I kept that to myself, unless I wanted to try to get some temporary relief by feeling good about having company in being bad.

Our priests and I weren't the only ones bound to keep "the seal of confession" about the dark side of the shadow we were casting. All of us seemed bound to keep it. It was a kind of unwritten agreement among us. It was our preferred way of coping with the negative side of our shadow.

> "Mum's the word."
> "Don't let the neighbors know."
> "Don't tell a soul."
> "Keep it to yourself."

"What happens in this family stays in this family."
"Not a word of this to anyone, you hear?"
"It's nobody else's business."

This was just a small part of the very long litany of solemn secrecy by which we invoked "the seal of confession" and protected the good reputation of our individual selves, our family, our neighbors, and our church.

An equally common way of coping with the dark side of our shadow was to pretend it wasn't even there.

"A shadow? What shadow? I don't see any shadow."
"A skeleton in *our* closet? You have to be kidding."
"She would *never* do a thing like that."
"Shadow? Go wash your mouth out. You're talking about the Catholic Church!"
"It never happened, I tell you. It never happened."
"I am *not* taking sides. There *are* no sides in a Catholic family."
"Would *I* do a thing like *that*? Come on. Get serious. I'm a Catholic."

When new guests would arrive at the therapy center in Jemez Springs one of the guys there would put on a special T-shirt to welcome them. The message written in bold letters across his chest read, "Denial is not a river in Egypt." It was so true it wasn't even funny. But it usually takes quite a while for most of us to recognize the River of Denial within us, and longer still for us to admit that it exists.

One of the more violent and destructive ways we had of keeping the River of Denial flowing through the Church that we were was to blame it all on somebody else. Although we didn't call it that, scapegoating was a very popular game among us. There was no limit to the number who could play, either. All we had to do to play was to identify the malevolent side of our shadow with some other person, family, religion or group, and to keep the benevolent side for ourselves. Of course, it was hard to do that without making our shadow much darker, but we didn't get into that. We wanted to keep it simple so that everyone could play. That is, *almost* everybody. The ones being blamed were a very important part of this game, but it wasn't a game for them. They became the black sheep, or the stinking goat, or the outcasts. Their function was to carry the dark side of our shadow so that the rest of us could feel pretty good about ourselves. When we'd go to church on Sunday, something about the mote and the beam would come up from time to time but most of us didn't make any connection with our game of "odd one out." We all seemed to need the mote, or the goat, or the black sheep, or the "odd one out." When the going got really tough all we'd have to do was to load them up with the whole dark side of our malevolent shadow and send them off into exile in the desert. Then we could be the One, Holy, Catholic People of God again, at least for a while. The odds in winning this game were really good, too. They were much better than in playing the numbers on the street.

At the time, I was much too active a part of this scapegoating game to be able to see it for what it was. Except for the radio program "The Shadow" that I used to listen to religiously every week, I had never even heard of the shadow. I thought the dark side of things was a human problem and that, thank God, the Catholic Church didn't have a dark side. Where I would ever find this impeccable Catholic Church that didn't have any people in it was a question that never entered my mind. I was still a long way from studying theology, and some of the theology I eventually studied only made this problem worse. How to reconcile my "perfect Church" conviction with my personal experience of the Church as my extended family, warts and all, was another detail I hadn't worked out. I was just collecting the raw data at the time; my interpretation of it would have to wait until much later.

But if I thought that entering a religious community and becoming a priest would keep me dry from the waters of the River of Denial for the rest of my life, I was gravely mistaken. As far as I could see, taking vows and being ordained didn't transform me or anyone else into another, impeccable species. We remained more or less human. We also continued to be nurtured under the benevolent side of Mother Church's shadow. That didn't mean that we left the games we had played as lay Catholics at home, however. We brought them with us wherever we went and continued to experience the dark side of our own and Mother Church's shadow, perhaps even more intensely than most.

When I look at the present and past history of the Catholic Church, mine was a relatively mild experience of the malevolent side of Mother Church's shadow. It was clearly minor league.

What I experienced at Jemez Springs, however, was a whole other story. There I lived and ministered in the dark side of Mother Church's shadow as I had never experienced it before. This was the major league. It obliged me to live, work, and meditate with the full scope of the paradox of the Church's two-sided shadow. Thank God I was supported in this work by the faith Mother Church herself had nurtured in me, by the beauty of a Spirit-filled place, and by the friendship and talent of a very gifted staff of psychologists. But basically, this was a solitary work that I had to do alone and I was blessed with the solitude in which to do it.

For me, the painful paradox at the center of my two-sided shadow work was how, by doing religious ministry, a person could lose touch with his or her own soul and be transformed from a marvelous minister into a miserable one.

In my experience, no one becomes a priest or a minister in order to make others miserable. I was the vocation director for our community for eight years and I never saw or designed a vocation publication that read anything like this:

> *"Why be miserable all by yourself? Join the Norbertines and become part of a whole community of miserable priests and brothers who have been carrying on this tradition for over eight hundred years. What's more we now have a very extensive Misery Outreach Program (MOP) which will allow you to embody the dark side of the Catholic Church's shadow by making hundreds of Catholic students, parents, and parishioners miserable too. Don't delay! R.S.V.P. today!*

That's just not how a vocation begins. It usually begins by meeting a marvelous minister in the benevolent shadow of Mother Church and wanting to be just like her or him. It begins with a dream, a hope, or a vision that, as an official minister nurturing and being nurtured by the People of God, you will be able to make a real difference in your own and others' lives. I know that's where it all began for me.

But then what happens?

What I see sometimes happening then is that, without even noticing it, some of us ministers slowly begin to walk in a very different way. We no longer walk in a creative way by continually moving from the challenges of ministering through the deepening practice of meditating to the Reality of the Mystery animating our lives and then back again through meditating to ministering more faithfully. Instead, we start walking in a destructive way by making three lethal moves. We start working compulsively because "there's so much work to be done." We stop meditating because "there just isn't time." Then we begin to compensate compulsively for our increasingly lonely and meaningless workaholic lives because "I deserve it." With that, we start going in a whole other direction. We start going from ministry to misery.

Thank God, not all of us go all the way on this journey. Mercifully, something happens along the way that wakes us up and puts us back on course. But if we overlook or disregard that moment of truth and continue to walk in this most destructive way, the River of Denial begins to flow freely through our lives and we begin to embody the darkest side of the Church's shadow in the most unfaithful, scandalous, destructive and abusive ways. This is how I personally began to experience and understand the most painful paradox of the shadow of Mother Church.

What I also see now that I didn't see at first was how Mother Church can, first unwittingly and then quite consciously, collaborate in this most destructive process. She does this by encouraging, nurturing, rewarding and recruiting workaholic ministers because of her urgent need for ordained, celibate, male priests at this time. When the addictive behaviors of her official ministers begin to multiply and embarrass her, the dark side of Mother Church's shadow begins to manifest itself. She starts playing the very same games that we played in our neighborhood by overlooking, covering up, and denying what's really going on. At this point, whether we admit it or not, the waters of the River of Denial and Codependence are at flood stage, and Mother Church and her miserable ministers are beginning to drown in them.

This shadow is more than dark enough, but it seems to me that it becomes darker still if the full extent of a miserable minister's addictive behavior becomes a public scandal. Then Mother Church often begins playing scapegoat to maintain her own "pristine" innocence just as we did in our families and neighborhood churches. She begins punishing, shunning, disowning, exiling, and effectively excommunicating the addictive ministers she formerly supported. To experience this is to experience an especially vicious, ruthless, and scandalous part of the dark side of Mother Church's shadow. This is the dark shadow's endgame, not only in the lives of individual wayward ministers but in the life of Mother Church herself. It's lethal.

To a great extent, this is the Church we were helping to rebuild one minister at a time in our ministry in Jemez Springs even though we knew full well that the project was way beyond our capability and resources. Maybe it was because I had spent some time in intensive care, but I began to see our whole ministry as a kind of psychological and spiritual cardiology. The heartbeat I began hearing in our guests—and in Mother Church whom they were representing—was one with which I was personally very familiar. It was a heartbeat that was compulsively fibrillating from ministry to misery without any meditative pause in-between. What we were doing as a staff was trying to create the environment and provide the support and conditions that, first of all, would allow our guests to hear and admit that their heartbeat was a potentially lethal one. Then we could begin working together to help their heart convert its beat back to a revitalizing one. Basically, this involved opening up a reflective or meditative space in-between ministry and misery that would restore the heart's salutary rhythm and put our guests in touch again with the Mystery that would animate their lives and ministry.

When this would actually happen, we would begin cheering and rejoicing just like my own cardiologists did when my heart finally converted to sinus rhythm. No wonder. We were witnessing a major conversion right before our eyes. It was a conversion that often required that our guest "bottom out" in denial first, and then get knocked off his high horse as Saint Paul was and go around blind for a while in what seemed to be the total darkness of his own and the Church's shadow. This is when I would begin hearing late night tears in the darkness, whether we were together in church or not. Then our guest might begin to see a glimmer of the light side of the shadow shining in the darkness and begin to celebrate the Mystery of what he was going through. When I would witness this, it was as though I could hear Mother Church singing as she stood in the vigil darkness before the light of the Easter Candle, "O happy fault. O truly wondrous night that gives us such a Savior." This is Mother Church's shadow at its best. It's the shadow of the life-giving Mystery in which she courageously lives and breathes and has her being.

What we really regretted as a staff was that we weren't able to work with our guests in a preventive way much earlier in their journey. We also deeply regretted that we couldn't work in a preventative way with the Church community and leaders as a whole before the dark side of her shadow took over. I knew that doing this kind of family systems work with the Church would be very delicate and much more complex. But my presumption was that the conversion of the community's heartbeat from a dysfunctional to a salutary one would involve a similar process as the one the individual ministers were going through. It would involve a major communal conversion. First, it would involve Mother Church's bottoming out in a crisis of denial. Then she might begin to catch a glimmer from the light side of her shadow shining in the darkness and begin to celebrate anew the Mystery of who she truly is and serves. The way I look at the priest crisis now, the Church is pretty far down the road into the first step of this process and the T-shirts I spoke of are still very timely.

It was out of these two regrets that I wrote an article for *America* magazine entitled, "Are We Killing Our Priests?" It took me six full pages to answer unequivocally: "Yes." Before sending the article to the editor I gave a copy of it to three of my friends on staff and asked whether they found my description of the problem we were working with to be accurate. They each said that it was. One of them added, "You don't think this will make any difference do you, Fran?" When I said, "No," he replied, "Good."

I may have spoken a bit too quickly in answering "no" to my colleague's question though. I knew that my article wouldn't immediately stop us as a Church from killing our priests. But I did hope that writing about it might raise the question in a way some readers may not have thought of before. I hoped that it might remind them that the Church is human and, without handing out T-shirts, that denial is not a river in Egypt. I also hoped that it might let them see that the underlying problem in the critical shortage of priests that we are currently experiencing is not one of a lack of manpower. It's primarily a problem of a lack of spiritual vision and courage that keeps us from looking at alternative forms of priestly ministry, even if the price for looking the other way is to do violence to persons. That's the difference I honestly hoped my article might begin to make—a difference in awareness.

A priest in the program once said to me, "Fran, I've been preaching the Paschal Mystery for twenty-five years. This year, I've been living it." That's what the present priest crisis in our family of faith is teaching me. It's teaching me to live the Paschal Mystery publicly by faithfully embracing both sides and the in-between of the communal Mystery that the whole Church is being called to live at this time. On the one hand, the benevolent side of our family's shadow—Yeah! On the other hand, the malevolent side of our family's shadow—Boo! And *in-between*, a deep river of amazing Grace flowing right through our family's heart—Wow!

When our greatly loved Archbishop of Santa Fe was obliged to resign and to go into hiding because of a sexual incident between him and two young women when he was a young priest, the local newspaper sponsored a telephone survey. It invited local Catholics to call in and simply press a designated number to indicate whether they would or would not accept the former Archbishop back as their leader. Seventy-five percent of those who called in indicated that they would accept the Archbishop back.

To my mind, this was the compassionate People of God speaking publicly right from their hearts. It was the *sensus fidelium*—the faithful's felt sense of how to handle the crisis. I would have liked it had the Church officials listened to the people rather than sending a repentant and inspired Church leader into exile.

At the height of this crisis I saw a television reporter on the evening news waiting at the door of a parish church to interview someone on this scandal as they came out of Mass. He put his microphone up to the face of an elderly Hispanic woman and asked her whether the Archbishop's actions had destroyed her faith.

"Destroyed my faith?" she replied. "I believe in *God*, not in the Archbishop." And she walked away.

The reporter was completely nonplussed. He began fumbling for words. Finally, he was able to manage something like, "Well, there you have it. And now back to the studio."

"'I believe in *God*'....Well, there you have it."

There you have it, indeed.

18

Becoming a Judeo-Christian

> *Salvation is from the Jews.*
>
> —John 4: 22

I've always wondered where my deep affection for the Jewish People comes from. My childhood neighborhood may have been a ghetto but it surely wasn't a Jewish ghetto. The only Jewish people I knew as a boy were the owners of our two neighborhood drug stores and the couple who ran the grocery store across the street. I remember as a child, when I would go to their store to get something for my mother, how kind and understanding the couple was in letting us run up a grocery bill each month until my father would get paid. Otherwise, I guess I lived in a Catholic ghetto.

Maybe my deep affection for the Jewish People came from my love of the Hebrew Scriptures, especially the Psalms, the Prophets, and the Song of Songs. It might also have come from how influential the writings of Rabbi Abraham Heschel and Martin Buber were in my spiritual and philosophical formation. I became familiar with the mystical tales of the Hasidic Masters a little too late for them to have been the source of my affection for the Jewish People, but they certainly brought it alive. That was true too of my friendship with Reuven Gold, a Hasidic storyteller with whom I led a couple of retreats.

I first met Reuven at a seminar on meditating, story-telling, and the Psalms that was hosted by a Lutheran seminary. The seminarians seemed to think that I was "way out" when I attempted to lead them in a *LifeProcess* meditation. At first I didn't think they heard me, but they heard me all right. They just refused to close their eyes or to take notes as the meditation progressed. Many of them also crossed their arms, which can make it rather hard to take notes, even if you want to. It can make it very hard to meditate, too. So, for what it was worth, we did a wide-eyed-no-notes-arms-crossed *LifeProcess* meditation. It was the first and the last one I ever did. It symbolized for me part of why I left the classroom, especially the seminary classroom.

If the seminarians thought *I* was "way out" I wonder what they must have thought about Reuven. He appeared with unkempt graying hair and beard in a loosely flowing, multi-colored, tie-dyed smock and began acting out Hasidic stories, telling them in a strange sing-song voice that seemed on the verge of breaking into song. At times it did, and Reuven would wind up singing a song in Hebrew. The seminarians must have thought that he was really "off the wall." As far as I could see, they didn't takes notes for him either. But I thought he was a great storyteller.

Walter Brueggemann, a well-known Lutheran exegete, followed the two of us by giving a very moving lecture on the Psalms of Lament that was enthusiastically received. Actually, I think it saved the day.

I don't think the seminarians knew what to do with a *LifeProcess* meditating Catholic priest, so at lunch they gave me a table at the other end of the dining room where I could be all by myself. When Reuven saw me there he came over and sat down. "What are you doing sitting here all alone blessing everyone who enters the room with your smile?" he asked. We were friends from then on.

There we were, two misfits having lunch together and telling each other stories. Maybe *that's* what attracted me to the Jewish People; so many of them have lived as misfits over the centuries, including the prophets. Maybe *that's* what attracted me to them. Even misfits need company.

Or maybe it was the Jewish storytelling. With Jews, telling stories seems to be a way of life. There's a story about a man who asks a rabbi, "Rabbi, how come you Jews always answer a question by telling a story?"

The rabbi answers, "That reminds me of a story."

Maybe that's what attracted me to the Jewish People. I love a good story, especially one with a spiritual punch line, but any good story will do.

One Sunday when the Scripture texts were about the universal calling of the Jewish and Christian Peoples, I began my homily with a story about a faithful old rabbi who died and went to heaven. Father Abraham threw the gate wide open for him and greeted him warmly.

"*Shalom*, Nahum," Abraham said, "*Shabbat Shalom*. I've been waiting for you." Then he put his arm around the rabbi and led him into Paradise.

As they entered, the rabbi noticed a crowd of people in the corner who were making a terrible din.

"Father Abraham," the rabbi said, "who are those people over there who are making so much noise?"

"Oh, don't let them bother you, Nahum," Abraham replied. "They're the Irish Catholics. They think they are the only ones here."

After Mass a big Irishman who looked like a linebacker followed me into the sacristy. "Father," he said shaking his head, "that homily really upset me."

"It did?" I asked. "Why?"

He looked me straight in the eye and said, "As soon as you said that the rabbi went into heaven I said to myself, 'Now, what in the world would a rabbi be doing in heaven?'"

That's what I call a good story. I only got away with it, though, because I have a face like the map of Ireland. Otherwise, it would have been very risky.

Anyway, life kept pointing me to my heartfelt connection with the Jewish People. Another way this happened was when I was a young priest. The word got out in Philadelphia that I was open to joining the rabbis in witnessing Jewish-Christian weddings. The couples started lining up and my students began calling me "the rabbi priest."

These weddings were often between a Jewish man and an Irish Catholic woman. The marriage preparation sessions I had with these couples were the best I've ever had in my life. The couples really had to search their souls together to discover what they shared at the spiritual level of their lives and how they would give it expression in their love for one another and for their children. Our conversations were marvelous. There was nothing legalistic or formal about them. They were heart-to-heart and life-to-life conversations. They also were a mini-ecumenical movement. That movement didn't stop with the couple, either. It extended to the two families as well. They almost invariably had difficulties with this kind of wedding, and in relating to those who were soon to become "the other side of the family." After working through all of that, finally being able to join the rabbi and the two families in celebrating the couple's wedding made me especially happy.

At one wedding reception I was seated at the head table next to an old rabbi whom I gathered was a patriarch of sorts. He was very upset by the whole celebration. He just couldn't bring himself to look at me or to speak with me. I tried to be as attentive to him as I could. I could feel how painful the celebration was for him.

When the couple got up to dance their wedding dance, the old rabbi couldn't take it anymore. He shook his head and said out loud so that I could overhear it, "It shouldn't be. It shouldn't be."

I turned to him and said, "Yes, Rabbi. It shouldn't be. But look, here it is. Here they are dancing together in love."

The rabbi turned his head and looked at me. Then he told me a story that this reminded him of.

Other heartfelt pointers to my connection with the Jewish People came when I saw the movie Schindler's List, which I did several times, or read Anne Frank's Diary, or Edith Stein's life, or many other books on the Holocaust. I was so deeply moved by them that I felt I actually belonged to this heroic People, or at least wanted to. It was the nature of their communal martyrdom at the hands of Christians that made me deeply realize that, for me, the Jews were and still are a Messianic People heroically living the Mystery of the Passover in public. It made me feel that, in some mysterious way, we are all being deeply blessed by their fidelity.

The fact that Jesus himself was a Jew and that I was deeply in love with him may well be the taproot of my affection for the Jewish People but, for some reason or other, I wasn't dwelling on that obvious connection at the time. I guess I was too busy wondering why in the world I was so attracted to the Jewish People.

When we had a life-size statue of Miriam, the mother of Jesus, carved for our parish church in Albuquerque, I overheard two elderly Hispanic women assessing it.

One woman, shaking her head, said to the other, "I don't like it."

"Why not?" the second woman asked.

"Because she looks like a Jew!" the other replied.

"She *is* a Jew," her friend answered.

End of conversation.

At any rate, eventually, I began to feel that I was being called to become a Judeo-Christian, just like the first Christians were. I'm a bit amused by it now but, at first, I took this calling quite literally. I began studying Hebrew with the help of a rabbi who was in spiritual direction with me, and went to see three rabbis about becoming part of their congregations.

As I spoke with the rabbis I could see that they had no idea of where I, as a Catholic priest, was coming from. Of course, my inability to explain where I was coming from didn't help much either. None of them seemed to think it was a good idea and, as I spoke to them, I began to have my doubts about it too. But two of them were kind enough to invite me to attend their synagogue service to see for myself. That was enough to convince me that joining a synagogue or the local community of Messianic Jews was not the form my Judeo-Christian stirrings wanted to take. I wasn't being called to add another whole set of formal Jewish religious rituals and rules to the whole set of very formal Catholic religious rituals and rules that I already observed. So the door closed on that, which made me think that there must be some other form that my stirring to become a Judeo-Christian wanted to take, and that it probably would be at a deeper level.

Studying Hebrew for a year was a good move in that direction. Right from the start, I had the sense that Hebrew is a sacred language. Studying it was a spiritual experience for me. I had always been moved by the beauty of Hebrew letters even when I didn't know what the letters meant. I just liked to look at them. It seemed to me that they each had a personality and strength of their own. When a couple of them got together, this strength was intensified. I also had a few favorite letters and words that I liked to write out for my self. I still do, but now I have some idea what they mean.

I didn't stay with studying Hebrew long enough to become fluent in it but by the end of a year studying it on my own, I was able to pray some of the prayers from the Hebrew Prayer Book. Praying like that made me feel that I had found at least one very fundamental way to honor my calling to become a Judeo-Christian and to be in communion with the Jewish People.

Long before I had a clear sense of this calling, I had an experience that kept pointing me in this direction. It may have been my first indication of how deep my affection for the Jewish People actually went. It came to me as a story while I was walking in the woods behind our Abbey outside of Philadelphia after having celebrated one of the Holy Week Masses. As I walked along, the story came to me verbatim, as though it were being dictated. This felt very strange. It actually frightened me. I knew the whole story was in me just as I had heard it, but I was afraid to mention it to anyone or to write it down. So I just walked with it and waited.

A few days later the story finally let me know that it wanted to be written down. I sat down right away and wrote it out word for word, just as it had come to me.

The Rabbi's Gift

There once was a famous monastery that had fallen on very hard times. Formerly its many buildings were filled with young monks and the church resounded with the chant. But now it was deserted. People no longer came there to be nourished by prayer. A handful of old monks shuffled through the cloister and praised their God with heavy hearts.

On the edge of the monastery woods, an old rabbi had built a little hut. He would come there from time to time to fast and pray. No one ever spoke with him, but whenever he appeared the word would be passed from monk to monk: "The rabbi walks in the woods." "The rabbi walks in the woods." And, for as long as he was there, the monks would feel sustained by his prayerful presence.

One day the abbot decided to visit the rabbi and to open his heart to him. So, after the morning Eucharist, he set out through the woods. As he approached the hut, the abbot saw the rabbi standing in the doorway, his arms outstretched in welcome. It was as though he had been waiting there for some time. The two embraced like long-lost brothers. Then they stepped back and just stood there, smiling at one another with smiles their faces could hardly contain.

After a while the rabbi motioned the abbot to enter. In the middle of the room was a wooden table with the Scriptures open on it. They sat there for a moment, in the presence of the Word. Then the rabbi began to cry. The abbot could not contain himself. He covered his face with his hands and began to cry, too. For the first time in his life, he cried his heart out. The two men sat there like lost children, filling the hut with their sobs and wetting the Word with their tears.

After the tears had ceased to flow and all was quiet again, the rabbi lifted his head. "You and your brothers are serving God with heavy hearts," he said. "You have come to ask a teaching of me. I will give you a teaching, but you can only repeat it once. After that, no one must say it aloud again."

The rabbi gazed at the abbot and said, "The Messiah is among you."

For a while all was silent. Then the rabbi said, "Now you can go home." The abbot left without a word and without ever looking back.

The next morning, the abbot called his monks together in the chapter room. He told them he had received a teaching from "the rabbi who walks in the woods" and that this teaching was never again to be spoken aloud. Then he looked at each of his brothers and said, "The rabbi said that one of us is the Messiah."

The monks were startled by this teaching. "One of us is the Messiah?" they asked themselves. "What could this mean? Is Brother John the Messiah? Or Father Matthew? Or Brother Thomas? Am I the Messiah? What could this teaching mean?" They were all deeply puzzled? by the rabbi's teaching. But no one ever mentioned it again.

As time went by, the monks began to treat one another with a very special reverence. There was a gentle, wholehearted, human quality about them now which was hard to describe but easy to notice. They lived with one another as men who had finally found something. But they prayed the Scriptures together as men who were always looking for something. Occasional visitors found themselves deeply moved by the life of these monks. Before long, people were coming from far and wide to be nourished by the prayer life of the monks, and young men were asking, once again, to live with the monks for a lifetime.

In those days, the rabbi no longer walked in the woods. His hut had fallen into ruins. But, somehow or other, the old monks who had taken his teaching to heart still felt sustained by his prayerful presence. They still felt sustained by his prayerful presence....

As I carried it around under my heart, this story became like a spiritual mirror for me. Almost every time I'd looked into it I seemed to see something new.

At first glance I saw that bringing hope to troubled communities like the Rabbi had done was how I wanted to spend my life. Later on, I saw that I was being called to live a much more solitary and intense prayer life that would put me more personally in touch with the Word and the Mystery. Still later, the story seemed to encourage me to give up lecturing and engaging in long debates and to teach by example, using few words with many implications. I was already living in a hermitage before I remembered how the story had mirrored me doing this long before it actually happened. Then I began to see that the Rabbi was a misfit too. Later still, I saw this story reflecting the painful divorce that my monastic community was going through and showing me how I was to react to it. At yet another time, it let me see that I was to embody the spiritual connection between Jews and Christians in the same simple way the Rabbi did. Later on, it assured me that "walking in the woods" was more my way of praying than constantly going to Church like the monks did. As a religious priest, I had to keep that quiet. Prior to that, the story had let me smile at the fact that even if the official leader gets the teaching all mixed up as the Abbot did, its power still finds a way to get through. Later, it gave me the great joy of actually seeing the hope this story had given me. I actually saw my brothers and sisters in the troubled monastery I had left "living together with one another as those who had finally found something and praying the Scriptures together as those who were always looking for something." What a blessing that was.

As I look in the mirror of this story now, I can see more clearly than I ever have in my life that, for me, the teaching that "the Messiah is among us" is not a rumor. It's a fact of life.

I still experience "The Rabbi's Gift" as pure gift. In a very deep way, it's the story I'm living. It's my Judeo-Christian story.

I once told "The Rabbi's Gift" to a fellow theologian as we were having lunch together. "That's a pretty good story, Fran," he said, "but you made one mistake in writing it. The Rabbi didn't say, 'One of you is the Messiah.' He said, 'The Messiah is among you.' If you corrected that mistake, it would be a much better story."

"Who am I to correct the Abbot?" I replied.

Anyway, in time, "The Rabbi's Gift" began popping up all over the place, even in Australia. I rejoiced in this. The story was taking on a life of its own. One of my good monk friends even told me as much. After I had given him a copy of the story, he asked me, "Did *you* write 'The Rabbi's Gift'?"

"Yes, I did," I replied.

"It reminds me of a line of Ogden Nash," he responded. "Yes, it's true I wrote it, but I'll kill you if you quote it."

Then he went on jokingly to complain about how many homilies he had heard all over the country that began with, "There once was a famous monastery which had fallen on very hard times...." "I thought if I heard it once more, I'd die," he added with a smile, "but thanks for the gift, anyway."

I was grateful for his comment. It kept me from telling the story in one of my homilies at that monastery which I surely would have done.

The first Google search I ever did was for "The Rabbi's Gift." I did it just to see if there would be any entries on it. Thirty-two hundred entries came up! Of course, they all weren't for the story. Some were for the Rabbi's Gift Shop, or gifts to get for your rabbi, or something like that. But many of the fifty or so first entries I looked at were about the story. One entry even let me know that a seven-minute movie of it was available. That was news to me. Another actually noted that the contact person had collected a hundred different versions of "The Rabbi's Gift." I could see the first ten for free. If I wanted to see the rest I would have to pay for them. I wonder what my monk friend who had had enough of "The Rabbi's Gift" would have thought about *this*!

As I looked at the first ten versions of the story I was struck by how different and original the variations on it actually were. One version made no mention of a monastery at all. In another version, the Rabbi came off like a psychoanalyst. He was looking in one of the monastery's windows, figuring out what was going on in there. Another version took place in a Hebrew school for Torah study. These different versions made me think it would be fun sometime to do a literary comparison of them, like the Scripture scholars do, to see how they may have been related to one another and to the original story. However, one thing was clear to me even from a first reading of these different versions. The oral tradition that generated them was alive and well. I was delighted to see that. It told me that the story now had a life of its own.

When I look in the mirror of "The Rabbi's Gift" now, I can see my whole journey toward becoming a Judeo-Christian reflected in it, including the decisive turn it took at the only reunion I remember our family ever having. My nephew Chuck gave each of us a copy of our family tree that he had been diligently researching for several years. It traced my father's side of the family back through six generations in the States to its roots in Germany in 1733. The name of the patriarch of the family was Samuel Dorff. He probably came to the States around 1750 where he fathered his first son, Jacob Dorff.

I was dumbfounded when I read this. It was hard to believe. In all of my searching to become a Judeo-Christian this had never even occurred to me. I actually *am* a Jew already. I have Jewish blood in my veins. Without even knowing it, I've been a Judeo-Christian all my life!

Given my long journey to become a Judeo-Christian, I was surprised how long it took me to assimilate personally the fact that I already was one. Without their even knowing it, my mother and father's wedding was one of those marvelous Irish Catholic-Jewish weddings I had celebrated as a young priest! If I had been in Germany as a child, I thought, I could have gone to a concentration camp instead of to a Catholic grade school. God only knows where I would have gone from there.

I don't know why, but just as I had felt when "The Rabbi's Gift" first came to me, I felt that I had to keep my Jewish heritage under my heart for a while until I fully realized the truth and the wonder of it. Then, like the old rabbi who sat with me at the wedding, it reminded me of a story I am now very pleased to tell.

When I look in the mirror of "The Rabbi's Gift" now, I'm able to say, "*Ich bin Jude.* I am a Judeo-Christian." I'm proud of it too, even though I had nothing at all to do with bringing it about. Like my life itself, I experience it as pure gift.

Now, at long last, I finally have come to know where my deep affection for the Jewish People comes from, and why I've always felt sustained by their prayerful presence.

19

Becoming a Catacomb Christian

> *How shall we get to the well*
> *now that it has been covered*
> *by the stones of the cathedral,*
> *now that it has been hidden*
> *by the passage*
> *of the centuries?*
>
> —Ira Progoff, *The Well and the Cathedral*

By our second year in Rome my fellow student, Roman, and I knew that we had to get our periodic tour guide service better organized. The key question involved in doing that was, when the Community's occasional American guests would visit, which one of us would be their guide to the Vatican Museum and which one was going to be their guide to the Catacombs?

Some questions answer themselves.

Roman loved history, especially the history of the European royal families and of the papacy. He would talk about some of those distinguished people in such great detail and with such affection and admiration that you would think that they were part of *his* family.

On the other hand, I knew little about the history of the Papacy and even less about the European royal families. But I had been attracted to the Catacombs from the moment I set foot on the Appian Way. I would visit them every chance I got. Each visit felt like a pilgrimage to me. I could feel these narrow winding tunnels lined with the dug out graves of early martyrs still carrying the atmosphere and the energy of a struggling, persecuted, extremely faithful and courageous People with a new vision for an increasingly decadent world. These underground tunnels were the sacred hiding places outside the walls of the City where the religiously persecuted could secretly meet with one another and their dead for prayer, burial, mutual encouragement and consolation, and an occasional Eucharist. As they led me deep down into the bowels of the earth, these Catacomb places took me back in time. They let me read the original rough, hand-carved Latin names and symbols that reflected the faith of the very first Christians and let me feel their courage first-hand.

I didn't see the connection at the time, but the more I got to know the history and politics of the institutionalized church the more deeply I felt that, although the edict of the Emperor Constantine stopped our being slaughtered and let us be accepted by the Roman society and come above ground as a People, we lost something very precious as a Christian community when we left the Catacombs. In really having to get organized as the religion of the Holy Roman Empire, we lost much of the character we had as a struggling, spiritually liberating, underground movement of misfits. I couldn't help feeling that we had lost much of the original charism and genius we had of being "in the world but not of it," and the courage we had been given to pay whatever price that might cost.

That reminded me of the story of the young pilgrim who was met by an elder of the community as he got off the ship that had carried him to this country.

"Did you come here to find religious peace and freedom, too?" the young man excitedly asked the elder.

"I did at first," the elder replied.

"You did at first?" the young man puzzled. "Then what happened?"

"Then we got into real estate," the elder matter-of-factly answered.

I still remember the face of an older nun who came to me after I had told this story in a retreat. It was a face of deep regret. As if she were talking to her self, she said, "That's what happened to us, too. We got into real estate." Then she slowly walked away.

The early desert mothers, fathers and monks seem to have felt the same way. Once they got a good look at the aboveground face of our Church, they headed for the heart of the desert catacombs and monasteries to continue the pristine witness of a Church of martyrs, outcasts, and visionaries. Through the moving wisdom stories, monasteries, and desert tradition of spirituality that they left behind, the richness of their journey gradually became a living part of the love I had for the Church of the Catacombs.

I didn't have to work hard at loving the Catacombs. For me, it was a case of love at first sight. It took me a lot longer, however, to recognize that I was a Catacomb Christian at heart. It first began to come to me gradually through my many visits to the Catacombs and through the anti-clericalism I had experienced in Rome and Paris. It then came to me as I explored the underground foundations of some of the most celebrated churches of Rome. Later it came hidden in my growing lack of interest in a dogmatic theology that was doggedly dedicated to defending an Empirical Church, and a clericalized theology that read like an erudite ecclesiastical newspaper with innumerable footnotes and no pictures. I knew that I had to learn to live with and repent for the pomp, pretense, triumphalism, arrogance, and legalism of my very human Church, just as I had to learn to live with and repent for my own. But I also knew that I couldn't live *from* there. I had to live from much closer to the bare-bones Catacomb faith of our Pilgrim People. That went down deep enough to let me commune with everyone without judging them or trying to convert them to our way of doing things. Paradoxically, recognizing this was a big part of the intense desire I began to feel to live in a more solitary and contemplative way. I'm now experiencing the hidden life that goes with that as a very real Catacomb.

For me, becoming a Catacomb Christian never meant making a sentimental, romantic journey back to the "good old days" of the Catacombs. We left the Catacombs for good in the third century and thanked God as we did. I left them seventeen centuries later when I departed from Rome. Having visited them so often and grown to love them so deeply I have never been able to forget them, but the Catacombs could never, ever, symbolize for me "the good old days."

For me, becoming a Catacomb Christian means living here and now from the deepest, simplest, hidden, underground depths of the faith with which God continues to bless me through the Church, even if that means living as a priestly misfit. I don't experience this as a *previous* step to be returned to and imitated. I experience it as the *next* creative step to be taken in my faith journey. For me, it's as though I'm being called to live from the crypt underneath the Church so that I can discover for my self what really goes on there and meet whoever else might be living from there, no matter who they are.

I didn't have to work hard to try to fabricate this image of living from the crypt of the Church. It came to me as all genuine images do, as a gift. It still comes to me that way in a recurrent dream of discovering the Church.

The dream usually starts with me all alone wandering around in a magnificent cathedral or in an old Abbey church or chapel with which I'm very familiar. I'm sometimes welcomed there by a solitary, silent, robed figure. Then I'm led, or find my way down, a stone staircase or through what feels like a cave, or a grotto, or the ruins of a wall, into a crypt of an ancient church that is beneath the church on the surface. I know immediately that this is a very sacred and mysterious place but it doesn't frighten me. If I came down alone then I sometimes meet an old, monk-like figure who seems to have been waiting for me to come. We never speak, but, through the silence, it feels as though he's sharing some of his wisdom with me. Sometimes this crypt-like church later leads to yet another underground church which feels even more mysterious and extraordinary. Even though I've been there in previous dreams, I'm always surprised and mystified to discover this deeper church. I never even suspect it's there. Every time I visit, it feels like the first time ever.

As I wake up, the deep atmosphere of this dream usually stays with me for a while. It has a very different quality from that of many of my other "everyday" dreams. It feels much deeper, much more expansive, and much more powerful and universal than I can ever say.

For the first time ever, three of these underground church dreams visited me in a little over a week's time. This made me feel that the dreams were urgently trying to tell me something. The figure who met me in all of these dreams and led me to the underground churches was my former abbot at Daylesford Abbey. I lived with him for a long while and served for many years on his Council. He was a very good priest and confrere and, as my Latin teacher for four years in high school, he was a major influence in my desire to become a Norbertine priest.

I knew that he wasn't one to put much stock in dreams but these dreams seemed to be telling me to get in touch with him anyway. So I wrote him a long letter in which I told him about my three dreams. In it, I described how deeply he had influenced my life and vocation; how much I admired how nobly he had led the community in the most trying times; and how grateful I was to know him.

I got a handwritten reply from him right away telling me that my letter had made his day and, in a very upbeat way, catching me up on what was going on with him and with the community at the Abbey.

In the last paragraph, however, the whole mood of his letter changed abruptly. It went something like this:

I'm convinced that if we don't abandon our whole lives totally to God, we have no future as a religious community.
Blessings,
John

These felt like very weighted words of wisdom to me. I cut them out, had them laminated, and placed them in my breviary so that they would always be with me at prayer. These were Abbot John's last words to me. They felt like an enlargement of the dreams I had shared with him and a hint concerning what my repeatedly visiting the underground churches might be all about. Abbot Neitzel died approximately a month later on Easter Sunday morning, just as he had hoped. It was his eighty-fifth birthday.

My dreams aren't the only way in which these underground church experiences come to me. They often come to me in meditation as well. The nice thing about that is that I don't have to wait until I wake up in order to record them. In my half-awake meditative state, I can record them right while they're coming to me.

What I'm beginning to realize now is that, ever since I left the classroom, I've been guiding people through the Catacombs of their own lives in spiritual direction and in the retreats I've been giving in meditative writing. While I make no mention of the Catacombs, it's as though we go together to the inner, underground places of our own lives. We discover for ourselves what's going on there and what might want to be brought back to enhance and animate the quality of our lives on the surface. Over the years, I've experienced this recurrent downward-upward, inward-outward journey to be amazingly energizing and creative.

During the past five years, what has powerfully connected this meditative journey with my experience of becoming a Catacomb Christian has been the week-long retreats of spiritual deepening that I've been leading for Evangelical ministers. These *Called Back to the Well* retreats originally came from the desire I had to move the ministry I'd been doing for ministers at Jemez Springs further "upstream." In this way I hoped to be able to help ministers develop a meditative lifestyle *before,* rather than *after,* they were burned out by their demanding work.

One of the amazing differences for me between this ministry and my previous one in Jemez Springs, however, is that I'm not leading these retreats just for Catholic priests and brothers. It turns out that I'm leading them primarily, if not exclusively, for Evangelical ministers from many different denominations. If, like Moses, I live to be one hundred and twenty years old, I will never take this gift for granted. Who would ever believe it? A Catholic priest like me being welcomed by these Protestant leaders to minister to them spiritually. And with no questions asked! I find this to be extraordinary.

During these intensive retreats in meditative writing we gradually find our way from the many cathedrals in which we minister, through our shared silence to the deep inner sources from which these cathedrals emerge and on which they stand. Then, following in the footsteps of the pilgrims who have gone before us, we gradually find our way back up to the surface of our lives with the vision and the energy to continue to do something creative in this world.

Along the way, something very mysterious often happens. We hardly get to know one another's names, much less our many denominations, differences, and backgrounds, before we enter the silence of the retreat. However, as we journey through that silence, alone and yet together, we begin to experience that, at the deepest level of our lives, we are undeniably One.

When, at the end of the week, the retreatants return from these silent depths to the surface of their lives they usually find that, try as they may, they can't adequately describe or explain the experience of deep communing that they have had. They also can hardly contain it. So they often attribute it to me, or to the prayerful presence of the Norbertine community, or to the awesome beauty of the desert, or to something else around them. As a Catacomb Christian, however, I can recognize that we've meditatively journeyed together to the underground place within us that is deeper than all of our differences. We've gone to the hidden temple on which all the cathedrals, mosques, chapels, synagogues, and temples are built. There, in the catacombs of our own lives, each of us has experienced the timeless Unity of Being that we all share. As often happens in the catacombs, these experiences come to us before their time. We don't yet know what to do with them on the surface of our lives. But we can't deny them.

As a young theologian I participated in many ecumenical meetings in which we spent our time theologically comparing our different creeds, codes, cults, histories, and projects in search of some common ground that we might possibly be able to share. As important as these deliberations were, I began to feel that they just didn't take us deep enough. But, at the time, I didn't know a way that could take us to the next step. I now know that the next step is a deeply meditative one. It's a kind of contemplative depth ecumenism that, as I experience it, can take us non-judgmentally not only to the common ground that is between us but, more importantly, to the common Ground that is *beneath* us. As Christians, it can take us to the Catacombs again and to the Ground of our shared Being in a most creative way.

As these experiences of deep communing continue to multiply for me, I find that I'm no longer alone in the Catacombs and that I never really was alone there. I've begun to experience a kind of anonymous

Catacomb Community meditatively tunneling their way beneath all of the religious, political, and cultural customs, structures, constraints and barriers of our times. My experience of this community leads me to believe that, if the truly catholic and universal aspirations of the Jewish, Hindu, Muslim, Buddhist, Indigenous, Christian, and other religious Peoples are ever to be realized, they will be realized here in the underground depths of persons, or they will not be realized at all. As this begins undeniably to happen in the Catacombs of our own lives, I can't wait to see the magnificently inclusive cathedrals that we will begin to build as a Catacomb People on the surface of our lives. That hope makes me feel doubly blessed and doubly privileged to be able to return to the Catacombs now in this completely new way and, as an old priest, to be invited, once again, to serve others as their Catacomb guide.

20

Becoming an Anonymous Priest

*To the Jews I became like a Jew.... To those outside the law
I became like one outside the law...I have become all things to all....*
—I Corinthians 9: 20-22

Do you have a past?

—Anonymous

When I first joined Ira Progoff over thirty years ago in giving Intensive Journal workshops all over the country, I immediately felt that this was a very priestly work. Of course I didn't dress like a priest to do it. I dressed like everyone else. We were doing a meditative work that, in order to be effective, had to be done in a neutral, non-denominational way so that seekers of whatever persuasion—and of no persuasion at all—could come together and discover for themselves what their lives were trying to become. I experienced it as a priestly work in the broadest and deepest sense of the word. I also experienced the methodology that Ira had developed as the most creative and comprehensive method for personal and spiritual development that I have ever come across. Through it, I was helping persons live an integrating life, which is a priestly work if I ever did one. It also was the most ecumenical work I've ever done. I experienced it as a sort of anonymous depth ecumenism.

Halfway through an eight-day workshop that I was leading, a distinguished-looking Spanish woman came up to me and said, "When this workshop began, I was puzzled that you hadn't mentioned God or Jesus at all. I wondered why a priest like you would be doing a neutral work like this. Now I know." With that, she walked away. I was relieved to hear that she had discovered for herself why I was doing this meditative work. That spared me the trouble of having to try to explain it. I found it awfully hard to explain to others' satisfaction why I was not only willing and able, but also fully committed, to be ministering to all kinds of people as an anonymous priest.

Another woman who spoke in a charming Southern accent put the question more bluntly. "Do you have a past?" she asked.

"A past?" I puzzled. "What do you mean?"

"Were you ever a priest?" she explained.

"I not only *was* a priest," I replied, "I *am* a priest."

"I knew it!" she exclaimed, as though she had just won the lottery.

Ira was having a very different experience. As the many Roman Catholic sisters who began attending his workshops would come up to him to read what they had written in their journals or to ask him a personal question, without even realizing it, they often called him "Father Progoff."

Ira got a real kick out of this. He'd jokingly say to me, "Fran, look at this. I'm being surrounded by priests and sisters. I'm becoming a real Judeo-Buddeo-Christian!" I suspected that might happen when I saw sisters and priests lining up to see Ira as the rest of us worked quietly. It looked to me like they were waiting in line to go to confession. In a sense, I guess they were. They were waiting to tell him something of real importance that was going on in the depths of their lives. So there we were, Father Progoff and Dr. Dorff, sharing a priestly work that was bigger than both of us.

I didn't think of it this way at the time, but the Intensive Journal workshops and retreats were a wonderful way for me to be a post-modern priest for post-modern persons. They were a type of moveable feast where all kinds of people could gather together to dedicate themselves to working meditatively with the facts of their own outer and inner experience, and to discovering the deep inner channels through which their lives were spiritually flowing.

As I would sit there leading the meditations and teaching participants how to use a journal as a tool with which to do this work, I sometimes felt like a bridge tender. It was as though I was sitting in the middle of a narrow footbridge greeting people as they crossed over from one side to the other. They are crossing it one by one, going in both directions, by attending carefully to the movement of their lives and, without judgment or comparison, describing that movement to themselves in writing.

One of the lines crossing the bridge is a line of deeply spiritual persons who have so equated their spirituality with formal religion that they have begun to overlook the deeply personal and spiritual dimensions of their everyday lives. I greet them as they cross over on their way to discovering the creative and more-than-personal depths of their own journeys.

The line going in the opposite direction is a line of persons who, because they are not religiously affiliated, have come to think that there is no spiritual dimension to their lives. I greet them as they cross over on the way to discovering, deep down, how spiritual their lives actually are. As I sit there greeting them, I marvel at these two lines of anonymous pilgrims, meeting, greeting, and supporting one another as they pass each other in the middle of the bridge. And I feel blessed to be with them.

At first, becoming an anonymous priest was pretty simple. All I had to do was to take off my Roman collar and my black suit, and dress like everyone else again. By doing that, I felt I'd have a good chance of being treated as a person, at least for a while. That gave me a break from being treated as an icon, or an official of a religious institution someone was either worshipping or having real trouble with. It also gave me a break from being a living reminder to someone that they hadn't been to church for a while, or hadn't made their Easter duty, or needed to go to confession. It wasn't so bad to get a great brief break from personifying guilt feelings for others, either. I know that's all part of being a priest—just as being treated with fear and deep suspicion is these days—but it feels good to get a brief breather from it now and then.

Although I've always been a priest at heart, taking off my collar also helped me avoid falling into the trap of equating my whole life with my priestly role in the Church. I know that's a very easy trap to fall into; priests can do it without even realizing it. My many little nieces and nephews were more than willing to pitch in to help me avoid that trap. They just took me as I was, and lovingly climbed all over me. They even trusted me with their hopes and dreams and asked me for a quarter. I kept thanking my sister and brothers for how my relationship with them and their children was enriching and shaping my life and ministry as a priest. In reply, they kept thanking me for how my relationship with them and their children was enriching the life of their families. They couldn't imagine themselves living celibately as I was and I couldn't imagine myself living maritally as they were. It was a perfect fit.

Before the Second Vatican Council, taking off my collar was much easier said than done. At that time, whenever I appeared in public, I was required to wear my "clericals." That included a white straw hat in summer and a black felt hat in winter, even though, apart from a football helmet, I had never worn a hat before in my life. In that outfit, just by showing up I could transform a very informal gathering into a very formal one without even trying. Except for other priests, I think I was the only twenty-some-year-old in the country wearing a white straw hat.

That was nothing, though, compared to the regulations that were in place when I first arrived in Paris. There, I was obliged to wear my white, medieval, monastic habit on the street unless I had the personal permission of the Cardinal to dress otherwise.

I had discovered right away that it's really hard to be singular in Paris. I had actually seen a woman walking down the street in her pajamas without even being noticed. But I know I would have been noticed in my habit. I would have looked like a very young Pope out of a very different era going for a stroll. So, one of the first things I did when I arrived in Paris was to get the personal permission of the Cardinal to dress otherwise.

But, for me, there was much more involved in becoming an anonymous priest than taking a break from the priestly role and not standing out in a crowd. I found that not wearing my clerical garb let all kinds of people who were disenchanted with the Church or religion or life feel more comfortable around me and freer to talk man to man—and woman to man—about what they were really going through. I met many people that way whom I never would have met in church or in the classroom, and our meetings often went to a deeply spiritual place. Being with these pilgrims became a kind of anonymous priestly ministry for me before I even had a name for it.

I then began to notice how being an anonymous priest was actually opening my eyes so that I could begin to see anonymous priests all over the place. I called them "marvelous ministers." Most of them didn't see themselves as marvelous, much less as ordained ministers or priests. But I saw them being ordained by courageously working through the brokenness of their own lives. Eventually, they wound up helping others who were having the very same trouble that they had had. They were very well qualified for that ministry, too.

A bishop wasn't ordaining these anonymous priests. Life was ordaining them. As I saw it, their ordination was often an "ordination by fire," too. But there they were, unselfconsciously ministering to prisoners after having spent seven years in the penitentiary themselves, or helping alcoholics off the street as part of their own recovery, or counseling couples after their own marriage almost fell apart, or teaching macrobiotic dieting to cancer patients after that diet had saved their own life, or caring for abused children after having been abused as a child, or volunteering to assist AIDS patients after caring for a brother who had died of AIDS. The litany is endless, and it celebrates the dedicated lives of this marvelous company of anonymous priests.

There are many things that make me marvel at these "marvelous ministers." One is that they come from every walk of life. Another is that I can't picture myself ever making their painful journey from misery to ministry through which most of them are ordained, or doing the heroic ministries they wind up doing. I know from walking with many of them personally that, at first, they couldn't picture themselves making this journey or doing this ministry either. The form their ministry finally takes for them often is beyond anything they could have imagined. It comes from Life itself. And there they are, being anonymous priests to other hurting persons.

As I got to know more of their stories from the inside, I began to realize that I had been witnessing a messianic ordination taking place. Of course, that doesn't mean that these marvelous ministers were becoming the messiah, any more than my ordination meant that I am the messiah. It means that their lives were being animated by a courage, a hope, and a love that is bigger than they are to do a creative work in the world that is beyond their own doing. As I marvel at their integrity and the creative form of their ministry, I'm actually marveling at the messianic quality of their lives. I also see them keeping the messianic secret even from themselves by the way they unselfishly went about doing good. These self-effacing priests are more anonymous than I can ever be. Theirs may well be one of the most creative ways of being a priest in the world.

My experience of witnessing anonymous priests being ordained by Life makes me think that the problem at the heart of the present critical shortage of priests in the Catholic Church is not really a lack of priestly vocations. It's a lack of spiritual vision. It's being unable to see the Messianic ordinations that are taking place all around us and to recognize, accept, and celebrate the many anonymous priests whom we already have in our community, just as the early Church once did. There is no denying that there is a shortage of officially ordained, male, celibate priests that is becoming more and more critical. But we don't seem to be able to see the many Messianic ordinations taking place that could help us solve that problem.

Later on, when I began thinking of the life of Saint Thérèse of Lisieux, who has been a close spiritual companion of mine ever since my novitiate days, my own experience of being an anonymous priest took another very big step.

I've always been fascinated by how—after all the prayer and energy she had put into being allowed, by exception, to enter the convent at fifteen years old—Thérèse was still not satisfied with just being the spouse of Jesus, a daughter of Carmel, and the mother of souls. In her spiritual autobiography, she reminds Jesus that she also wants to be a priest, an apostle, a martyr, a doctor of the Church, a crusader, a prophet, a wandering preacher, and a missionary to every single country and island on the earth "from the first day of creation to the end of all time." She also wants to imitate the humility of Saint Francis by remaining a layperson rather than becoming an ordained priest. She honestly admits that she's having a little trouble working out the details of how all of these desires fit together. In fact, she says that these conflicting aspirations are a real martyrdom for her. To me, she's starting to sound an awful lot like one of our many anonymous priests.

Thérèse then turns to Saint Paul for help but finds that, at first, he doesn't help at all. In his First Epistle to the Corinthians Saint Paul reminds her that, as the Body of Christ, the Christian community is just like our own body. It's not just one big eye acting as if it were the whole body, or one big head thinking that it can live without all the other parts of the body. No, just like our own physical body, the Christian community is a living organism made up of many different members caring for one another in many different ways. No one person is the whole Body, or all the parts of it.

This teaching doesn't satisfy Thérèse at all. She can't recognize herself in any one particular part of the Body of Christ that Paul mentions: apostles, prophets, teachers, miracle workers, healers, assistants, administrators, those who speak in tongues, or those with the gift of interpreting tongues. She still wants it all! She wants the gift of every single vocation God can give her. So she reads on, and Paul's powerful Ode to Love finally gives her the key to the vocation she's been looking for.

Set your hearts on the greater gifts.

Now I will show you the way which surpasses all the others.

If I speak with human tongues and angelic as well but do not have love, I am a noisy gong, a clanging cymbal. If I have the spirit of knowledge and comprehend all mysteries, if I have faith great enough to move mountains but have not love, I am nothing. If I give everything I have to feed the poor and hand over my body to be burned but have not love, I gain nothing.

Love is patient; love is kind. Love is not jealous, it does not put on airs, it is not snobbish. Love is never rude, it is not self-seeking, it is not prone to anger; neither does it brood over injuries. Love does not rejoice in what is wrong but rejoices with the truth. There is no limit to love's forbearance, to its trust, its hope, its power to endure.

Love never fails. Prophecies will cease, tongues will be silent, knowledge will pass away.... There are in the end three things that last: faith, hope, and love, and the greatest of these is love
   —I Corinthians, 12:30–13:13

This passage lets Thérèse see that all of the gifts she desires are nothing without love. It lets her realize that, as a body, the Church must have a heart. It must have a heart that is on fire with love and that unites all the other members of the body and keeps them alive. "Finally, I realized that love includes every vocation, that love is all things, that love is eternal, reaching down through the ages and stretching to the uttermost limits of earth." That's what she was really asking for!

Beside herself with joy, Thérèse exclaims "—*My vocation is Love!*... in the heart of the Church, my Mother, *I will be Love!*...Thus shall I be all things and my dream will be fulfilled."

I hadn't read this powerful description of self-discovery in years, but I had been carrying it around in me ever since I first came upon it. From time to time it would come to mind again, seemingly for no reason at all. Whenever it did, it pleased me. It connected me personally to Thérèse and to her refreshing "bring it all on" attitude that I don't think I have had since I was a teenager. It also made me wonder about what divine calling was at the heart of all the things *I* was doing and desiring. Being a priest has this character for me, especially as it expands into being an anonymous priest for everyone. So does being a philosopher and a theologian and a teacher in the deepest sense of these words. So does being a Judeo-Christian and a Catacomb Christian. In a surprising way, so does being a misfit.

Both feeling like a stranger in a strange land and being called to live in a more solitary and contemplative way have this deep character for me, too. So does my ongoing "experiment in loving." That "experiment" now feels like an inner pilgrimage to the Loving that grounds all of my longing and loving and is beyond all telling. So what's the call that's underneath all of these "callings"?

When Thérèse's description of the gift of her deepest divine calling came to mind again a few years ago, it eventually led me to feel that beneath all my callings, I'm being called in a similar way as she was. I'm being called to be Loving in the heart of the world.

I had no sooner realized this was my deepest call than a lot of things began clustering around it and rooting themselves in it. Among them are all of my other vocations: Teilhard de Chardin's experience of celebrating *Mass on the World* and discovering Fire for the second time; my sense of the environment being a guru; my growing passion for working and praying for the nonviolent unity and leadership in Spirit and action of all the religions in the world; and my sense that this deep divine calling of being Loving in the heart of the world is what the whole Church is being called to be by the Word of God, the Second Vatican Council, and the appallingly divisive and violent signs of our times.

Like Thérèse, I was having a little trouble, though, working out how all of this, and much more, fits together, until I realized that I didn't have to bother to work it all out. In a very personal way, I experienced this vocation already being realized by God at the deepest level of my Being. It is God Who is Loving at the heart of the world. If that's what I really want to be, then I'm being called to be One with God. In that most anonymous way of all, I will then be able to be all things to everyone and, like the Loving God of the Exodus, no one will see my footprints.

This is the vocation that's now at the heart of my life as an anonymous priest. I deeply believe it's the vocation I share, not only with every Christian, but also with every single person in the world. I believe that the life of our Whole Body depends on our all becoming "Loving in the heart of the world."

21

Seeking Wisdom Side-by-Side

That all may be one....
—John 17: 21

*A*s we dedicated the new church of our Priory in the desert just outside of Albuquerque, New Mexico, we sang, "All are Welcome," a rousing hymn by Marty Haugen, that struck me as prophetic from the very first time I sang it. Its last two verses are:

> *Let us build a house where hands will reach*
> *Beyond the wood and stone*
> *To heal and strengthen, serve and teach,*
> *And live the Word they've known.*
> *Here the outcast and the stranger*
> *Bear the image of God's face;*
> *Let us bring an end to fear and danger:*
> *All are welcome, all are welcome,*
> *all are welcome in this place.*
>
> *Let us build a house where all are named,*
> *Their songs and visions heard*
> *And loved and treasured, taught and claimed*
> *As words within the Word.*
> *Built of tears and cries and laughter,*
> *Prayers of faith and songs of grace,*
> *Let this house proclaim from floor to rafter:*
> *All are welcome, all are welcome,*
> *all are welcome in this place.*

We sang this song with all our hearts even though, as a prophetic song, it's coming before its time. As a community, we have been singing songs like this for two centuries but we still haven't been able to realize the all-inclusive Unity and Peace for which we so deeply long. In light of religion's current and long-standing history of being a source of prejudice, injustice, division, terrorism, violence and war, we may be tempted to give up singing this song. But I think that these times make it especially urgent that as a People we continue to have the courage to keep singing this song with all our hearts until we can discover creative ways of letting its faith-based vision come true. This song of deep communing describes a lifework that we know we can't do without God and that God won't do without us. When I see this song being realized, even in the most modest ways, I feel that I'm caught up in a miracle unfolding before my eyes that fills me with praise and thanksgiving.

Since this song of inclusive communing can't yet be fully realized in our church, our little community resolved that our new spirituality center would be a place where this could happen. All the while that we were building the library and planning its dedication, it was as though under our hearts we were singing with one voice, "*All are welcome, all are welcome, all are welcome in this place.*"

We decided right from the start that our library would not be just for us. It would be a private library open to the public. It would also be the only library in New Mexico specializing in the theology and spirituality of multiple religious traditions. In light of that, we wanted to do much more than dedicate just the library building. We wanted to dedicate *ourselves*, and anyone else who would join us, to an inclusive way of living. So we took our time. We set aside the whole year as the Year of Dedication and invited seekers from every religious tradition to join us in seeking Wisdom side-by-side in mutual respect and Peace.

Each month of the Year of Dedication we extended an open invitation to everyone we could to attend a meditative morning in which a local spiritual teacher would share a spiritual perspective and practice with us from within her or his own religious tradition. The presenters included a woman rabbi; a contemplative Anglican pastor; a Buddhist meditation teacher; an esteemed evangelical minister, mediator, and ecumenist; a Native American woman from Acoma Pueblo who teaches Pueblo languages and cultures at the University of New Mexico; a Catholic woman scripture scholar; and several other locally known Catholic spiritual teachers. The year concluded with a sacred concert by *de Profundis*, a celebrated men's *a cappella* ensemble from Albuquerque.

The response to these offerings was overwhelming. It was beyond anything we had dared hope for. We had never met half of the people who participated. This also was the first time we had used our worship space in the multipurpose way for which we had originally designed it. As we did, I could hear our song of dedication echoing from floor to rafter, *"All are welcome....all are welcome.... all are welcome in this place."* It was as though we were being given a foretaste of the wonderfully inclusive experiences of "seeking Wisdom side-by-side" that are yet to come.

As we welcomed our guests, we shared our vision with them and told them that we saw them personally dedicating our library by their presence with us. We also invited them to visit the library and take out a few books if they'd like, which many of them did. As our guests entered the library, the dedicatory plaque that greeted them at the door carried the prayer that Jesus prayed at the Last Supper, *"That all may be one."* Walking up the entry way that leads to the great sunlit main room of the library, they passed through the story of "The Rabbi's Gift" as it is reflected in six of a series of paintings by Sheila Keefe. These paintings include two that I find especially moving. One portrays the Rabbi and the Abbot sitting together before an open Bible, wetting the words "That all may be one" with their tears. The other portrays the Abbot's heart opening as he receives the Rabbi's teaching, "The Messiah is among you."

I had originally thought that our series of meditative mornings would lay the foundation for "seeking Wisdom side by side" with all kinds of spiritual pilgrims. But in the course of the presentations I began to realize that much more than that was happening in our church. As I experienced us peacefully sharing diverse spiritual perspectives, meditative practices, and our personal religious questions and convictions, I realized that we weren't just laying a foundation for *future* spiritual communing.

We were actually spiritually communing by seeking Wisdom side-by-side *here and now*. What's more, this experience was being hosted and facilitated by a Roman Catholic religious community in a Catholic Church. The experience was beautifully summed up for us in the *all-inclusive* spirit and language of sacred music of the *de Profundis* chorus singing from the deep place within us all.

We designed our worship space as a church within a church. It is a circular kiva being embraced by the arms of a Cross. The kiva is an underground sacred ceremonial space of the Pueblo Peoples that symbolizes for them the deep place from which they originally came. In our church, the kiva is symbolized by a thin white brick circle on an earth-colored floor and by four wooden arches that, with the grace of a double rainbow, reach up from the floor toward the skylight above the altar. Given this architecture, I was moved to tears by the way that the Pueblo professor concluded her presentation of the spirituality on the Pueblo Peoples. She asked us all to form a "Friendship Circle" by standing on the white brick circle while she and a Pueblo Elder called from the audience stood at the center and blessed us in their own beautiful language. Then she and the Elder went from person to person wishing us Peace. We all peeled off one-by-one and followed them around, wishing everyone else in the circle Peace until all that was left was the empty Kiva in the Cross and "*All are welcome....all are welcome....all are welcome in this place*" echoing from floor to rafter through the church.

Our worship space will never again be the same for me. Now, whenever I sit alone in our church, I feel that I'm sitting in a sacrament of hoped-for Unity. It's not only a sacrament of the Eucharistic Presence of Christ among us that we celebrate here every day. It's also a sacrament of the graced communion of the spiritual pilgrims from different religious traditions joining us in dedicating our library and our selves to "seeking Wisdom side-by-side." I still feel sustained by their peaceful presence in this place.

This experience leads me to think that what we need now in order not to lose heart and to realize the deep communion we long for is not just continued top-level theological meetings among the leaders of our different religious traditions. What I think we need now is to experience personally, in a concrete, grassroots way, the marvelous Mystery of spiritual communing that is already at work deep within us. As these experiences multiply, they will carry with them the vision, the courage, and the wisdom that we need to transform our different religious traditions into channels for Peace and Communion in a badly broken world. God willing, our library and our church will be places where pilgrims can have inclusive experiences of this kind.

In my keynote presentation for the Year of Dedication Series, I underlined with our guests the great difference in seeking spiritual communion between viewing our various traditions as separate religious *products* or things, and experiencing them as a deeply shared spiritual *process*. I described how I began to make this shift personally when I lost interest in my early ecumenical efforts to piece together the jigsaw puzzle of our diverse codes, cults, and creeds in an analytic and cognitive way in search of some common ground. That cleared the way for me to devote myself to seeking communion by learning how to walk gracefully in a Sacred Way with pilgrims of different religious traditions and of no religious tradition at all. After I described what I experience to be the art of walking in a Sacred Way that I believe all spiritual pilgrims share, we spent the rest of the morning meditatively trying it out. We concluded our session by sharing comments, questions, and some of our personal spiritual experiences that came from our meditative practice. The morning was pure gift.

Our Year of Dedication gave me yet another important gift. I knew right from the time I began teaching theology that my dissertation would be my first and last *magnum opus*. I knew that I was being called to be a teacher and not to be a research scholar. In spite of that, I've always felt that I've been somewhat remiss in not producing a theological tome, or even a series of tomes, that would be so profound that even my colleagues would have a hard time understanding them.

Our Year of Dedication relieved me of this misgiving. It let me appreciate much more than I ever had before that being part of a religious community involved in the challenging work of founding a new, inclusive, Norbertine Abbey is a way in which I have been doing theology all along without even realizing it. My *magnum opus* has been helping in a communal work of envisioning, designing, and building a place of spiritual beauty and shared seeking where all are welcome. As I experience it now, this has been a work of grace and a major theological enterprise. The fact that I haven't even realized that until now strikes me as strangely appropriate.

Actually, my keynote presentation summed up for me, in a very simple way, what I experience to be the underlying movement of my whole life of living and helping others to live gracefully with a restless heart. By walking in a Sacred Way, I feel that I am joining a host of unseen spiritual pilgrims who are seeking Wisdom side-by-side and courageously living creatively in a broken world.

> *As I realize this*
> *I realize as well*
> *that in all of this inner journey*
> *I have been walking in a Sacred Way.*
> *In all of this inner journey*
> *I have been walking in Peace*
> *through the facts of my life.*
> *I have been walking*
> *with inner attentiveness*
> *to all that Life would teach me.*
> *I have been walking*
> *in loving kindness*
> *with the quiet Presence*
> *and with all who share*
> *the Garden of Peace.*
>
> *I know I can continue this journey*
> *by walking in a Sacred Way*
> *through all the work I have yet to do*
> *on the surface of my life.*

*I know I can continue this journey
by walking in a Sacred Way,
by working in a Sacred Way,
by loving in a Sacred Way,
by living in a Sacred Way
on the surface of my life....*

*I must leave the Garden now,
and whatever comes to me at this moment....
whatever comes to me,
in whatever way it comes to me,
I simply record it here
to mark the place of my return,
to mark the place of my return,
In the Silence... In the Silence...*
    —The Flowering of the TreeCross

22

Getting to Know My Soul

The soul?

The soul is a peregrine falcon
with sharp talons, a beautiful breast,
and a piercing gaze
that cuts you to the quick.

We keep her in a bird cage
in the basement of the house.

We tried to take her to church
on Sunday morning
but she refused to go.

Perhaps it's just as well.
She'd only disturb the service.

She wants to fly free,
to perch on the top of the tallest tree,
to survey the world from the clouds
in soaring gyrations,
to glide and dive,
and chase angels around the heavens.

She wants to hunt
—yes, hunt!—
for what she most desires.

Now we can't have that,
can we?

> *So we keep her in a bird cage*
> *in the basement of the house,*
> *and try to forget about her.*
>   —Last Night I Died

This poem came to me as I was hiking on a beautifully sunny day in the Ventana Wilderness in Big Sur, California. It was as though an inner voice broke the wilderness silence and introduced me to my soul. I listened as I hiked along and stopped from time to time to write down what she was saying so that I wouldn't forget it.

Even though this poem came to me as a complete surprise and I was very grateful for it, its description of the soul didn't surprise me at all. I'd been walking with this image of the soul as a peregrine falcon ever since one paid me a surprise visit about a dozen years earlier.

One morning, I was sitting at the table reading in Siloam, the hermitage I had just built on the edge of our Abbey grounds outside of Philadelphia. It was a very still spring day with a hush about it that felt as though it was waiting for something. Suddenly, I heard a strange scratching noise coming from within the wood burning stove. Then everything was quiet again. I no sooner got back to my reading when the scratching started again and then stopped. This went on a couple of times.

Finally, I tiptoed over to the stove and carefully opened its iron door. There, in the doorway of the stove, stood a magnificent peregrine falcon looking right through me with her piercing gaze. What a regal bird!

We stood there just looking at one another for a while. Then she flew into the hermitage and perched on the railing of the loft above. From there, she had a commanding view of the little cabin and a great perch from which to keep a close eye on me.

I would have liked to have her company for a little longer, but I figured she must be feeling trapped in the hermitage. So I opened the door so that she could fly out and went back to my reading. The falcon didn't move at all. We sat there silently together for the better part of an hour.

I still find it impossible to describe the atmosphere created by the presence of the falcon. It was very intense and highly charged. It felt like I was sharing the space with a very special consciousness or, better yet, that a very special consciousness was sharing the space with me. And that was it. No words. No images. No big insights. Just the falcon's gaze and the intensity of the shared silence.

Before I knew it, it was time for me to go up to the house of prayer to meet with several retreatants, so I said goodbye to my guest and left the door open so that she could find her own way out.

When I came back to the hermitage later to fix myself some lunch the place felt empty. Before closing the door, however, I climbed up to the loft just to make sure that she had found her way out. There she was, clinging for dear life to the corpus on the cross above my bed and looking right through me just as she did before. As brief as it was, this was a very special encounter. I can still feel it. It was like coming face to face with my soul.

Then, as if she knew the door had been open all along, the falcon swooped down and flew right out. When I followed her outside to see if I could catch one last glimpse of her, there she was perched on the top of the tallest tree as if waiting to say goodbye to me. She lingered there for a moment, looked around, and then flew away.

I spent the rest of the day in the penetrating presence of my silent guest.

The soul?

The soul is a peregrine falcon
With sharp talons,
A beautiful breast,
And a piercing gaze
That cuts you to the quick.

I was delighted when the falcon paid me another surprise visit in this poem, but the image of the falcon no longer surprised me. It felt like the return of a very old friend.

As a dedicated bird watcher, I'm very pleased by the image of the falcon. I love the sound of her name, "peregrine," and the rich Latin overtones it has of "pilgrim" or "wanderer." I'm pleased to know that she's been making a remarkable comeback from being nearly extinct. I'm also struck by the fact that she can be found almost all over the world, which isn't true of many other birds. I also like the fact that this image of my soul came to me as a gift. It wasn't something I just thought up on my own. I'm touched, too, that the falcon came to meet me in Siloam, since I had originally built the hermitage as a place where I could get more in touch with my soul. It really pleases me as well that she chose to enter the hermitage through its centrally-located hearth like a falcon on fire. And the way she flies! She's clearly an image of my soul.

As important as the "pilgrim" falcon's visit was for me, I didn't have to wait until then to be introduced to my soul. I didn't always have an image or a name for her, but I don't think there ever was a time in my life when I wasn't aware of my soul's presence. The images and the names came much later. In fact, when I started getting serious about philosophy, theology, and psychology, names for the soul just kept coming whether they expressed my own experience of the soul or not. At that stage in my journey, studying these disciplines wasn't really about getting to know my own soul. It was more about learning all the different names scholars had given the soul so that I could hold an intelligent conversation about it.

Meanwhile, on a more meditative level, I kept on getting to know my own soul better and better. There seemed to be no end to it. The images of my restless heart and of my being a Judeo-Christian, a lover of God, an image of God, a temple of the Spirit, a lover of Wisdom, a lover of Beauty, a lover of Peace and Unity, an anonymous priest, a hermit, and a misfit with a certain affection for the peregrine falcon were all part of the gradual unfolding of my deepening relationship with my soul.

As I look at it now, it surprises me though that I didn't have more trouble with the diversity of this litany of images. As a student and a young teacher I spent a lot of time advocating clear and distinct ideas and maintaining, together with the whole scholastic tradition, the non-negotiable principle of contradiction in all things. From that perspective, the soul can't be a misfit *and* a falcon at one and the same time. It's unthinkable.

My relationship with my soul, however, just kept exploring the unthinkably opposite things that my soul can't possibly be but actually is. Our relationship was clearly moving along on another level altogether where, whether it boggled my mind or not, my soul wasn't having any trouble at all identifying with some very different symbols all at the same time.

Something that helped me to move along more gracefully in our relationship—and to communicate that movement more effectively to students and retreatants—was when I began to realize that the soul loves to make faces. So did I when I was a little child. One of the games my little brother, Bobby, and I used to love to play as children was "making faces." We would sit on the kitchen floor facing each other while my mother was cooking supper and take turns trying to top one another with the different faces that we could make.

When she had had enough of it, my mother had a surefire way of calling this game to a halt. She would just quietly say, "Francis and Bobby, stop making faces, or one of them may get stuck and you won't be able to change it."

As my experience of the spiritual journey led me to develop a more dynamic and developmental approach to doing philosophy, theology, and psychology, I began to realize that my soul loves to make faces too—faces that reflect right where she is at any given time in her journey. These faces are much subtler than the ones Bobby and I used to make as children. Although they are reflected outwardly as well, I see them primarily as inner faces. Taken together, they embrace and express the basic underlying movement of my whole life. I also see them changing as I move along, just as, whether I'm aware of it or not, the outward faces I make keep changing. A big difference is that I can't see the changing faces of my soul in a mirror: I have to learn how to feel the difference between their inner quality and shape. It's like learning an inner kind of Braille that helps me get to know my soul in a most touching way.

As I look back over the journey that my soul and I have made together, the first face I think that I was aware of her making was the face of "Doing-it Confidently." It took me quite a while to recognize that this wasn't the only face my soul could make. As my confidence continually turned into over-confidence, I began to recognize another face of my soul. It was the face of "Letting-Go Trustingly." This was a very different face from "Doing-It Confidently." It was a face that invited me willingly to give up my need for control and my unconscious assumption that I was omniscient and omnipotent.

I think it took me even longer to recognize the next face that my soul began making for me. But gradually I began to recognize the almost shapeless shape of my soul's face of "Letting-Be Hopefully." Part of why it took me so long to recognize this face was that as a younger man, no matter what happened, my motto was "Moving Right Along...." By contrast, in making her "Letting-Be Hopefully" face, my soul was inviting me to stand completely still and wait for her to make the next move. As benevolent as it was, I found this face to be pretty scary. It could feel like staring into a vacuum and wondering if anything could ever come from such emptiness. This is when I would be most tempted to lace up my combat boots and start resolutely marching backwards.

If I kept living with the face of "Letting-Be Hopefully," which would usually be just a little longer than I could possibly endure it, my soul would begin making yet another face. Right from the middle of this vacuous experience of awkward in-betweens, I would begin to see her making the face of "Letting-Grow Lovingly." This face reflects the joy of discovering a new hope, dream, inspiration, or project. It also is tinged with misgivings about how this inner vision is going to be realized in the outside world. But, on the whole, the soul's face of "Letting-Grow Lovingly" is a relaxed, relieved, deeply animated face. It's like the face of springtime coming on the heels of a long winter of waiting. When I see my soul making this face, it lets me get to work again with a confidence that I know comes from Someone else.

When the face of "Letting-Grow Lovingly" becomes well established, I'm tempted to think that I've completed this challenging journey. I'm finally home free and can settle down for good. This is when my soul begins making a much more subtle face on the other side of the joy and wonder of these creative beginnings. I eventually came to recognize this as my soul's, "Letting-Flow Gracefully" face. This face encourages me to keep following my soul's lead. It reinforces how my soul doesn't like to go around with just one face. She likes to keep making faces so that none of them get stuck along the way. If I don't try to take over, she lets one face just flow into another with a spontaneous rhythm, freedom and grace that amazes me. That leads me to believe that, "Letting-Flow Gracefully" is the face that underlies all the other faces that my soul makes. One of my greatest joys these days comes from following this gracefully changing face. It makes me feel that, without knowing exactly how, I'm actually moving with the deep Mystery of how my Life creatively unfolds.

If the soul had given me a T-shirt every time I've found myself in this Letting-Flow Gracefully place in the journey, I would have a closet full of T-shirts by now. They would all have the same message on them, too. They would all read, "Going with the Flow." That wouldn't mean following the crowd, either, but "Here we go again!" It would mean that I was finally learning to recognize the recurrent cycle of faces that my soul keeps making for as long as her journey into freedom and creativity lasts. In other words, my T-shirts would all read, "Bon Voyage!" These five faces of the soul can be painful and challenging at times but I still see them as the "Good News" faces of my soul.

It would be nice if I could say that I discovered that these five faces are the only ones that my soul can make, but I can't honestly say that. I discover this again and again whenever I refuse to follow my soul's stirrings and try to drown them out by insisting on "doing it my way." That's when my soul begins, once again, introducing me to the

"Bad News" faces she makes when I start taking the road from freedom into slavery.

It all begins quite innocently. I get very attached to my soul's "Doing-It" face. I get to like it so much that it makes the soul's face of "Letting-Go" look stupid to me. I self-confidently figure that, whatever I'm being called to do, my track record proves that I can take control of it and do it on my own. The impossible will just take me a little longer.

I now recognize that's exactly how my soul's initially admirable face of "Doing-It" begins to change into her increasingly rigid face of "Something-to-Prove." As the fallout begins to come in from my going around all the time with my "Something-to-Prove" face on, I find that I begin to need a lot more psychic and spiritual closet space to hide the negative outcomes, not only from others, but particularly from myself. So I start looking for a dump for all my toxic waste.

That's when my soul begins making her extremely guilty face of "Something-to-Hide." I usually have a devil of a time trying to cover up the nervous smile of this face, especially with those who have some feel for the soul's many faces. They seem to look right through me as the falcon did. That's a very uncomfortable feeling when my soul is making its "Something to Hide" face.

As my soul's "Something to Prove" and "Something to Hide" faces begin to blend into one another, they seem naturally to multiply the number and magnitude of fears they are forcing me to live with. To mention just a few, there's the fear of failing; of losing face; of losing control; of being exposed; of being thought poorly of; of reprisal. There's also the fear of being punished by life in some unknown way, of being vulnerable, or unloved, or pitied, or lost; of facing the Unknown, or dying and the fear of "Letting-Go Trustingly," "Letting-Be Hopefully," "Letting-Grow Lovingly," and "Letting-Flow Gracefully."

This is when my soul's face of "Something-to-Fear" no longer comes and goes, as it ordinarily does in my life. It gets stuck and becomes my dominant way of facing—or not facing—life and what's really real. Then all that I do becomes "fear-based" as they say.

As I have become more familiar with my soul's faces of

"Something-to-Prove," "Something-to-Hide," and "Something-to-Fear," I began to recognize them as her "Bad News" faces. They are the sad, sorry faces my soul keeps making as I insist on continuing my journey farther and farther into slavery.

I now can see how these "Bad News" faces are actually the shadow side of the soul's "Good News" faces. I can see how, in making her face of "Something-to-Prove," my soul is inviting me to let her make the face of "Letting-Go-Trustingly," a face which increasingly has nothing to prove to others *or* to myself. In making her face of "Something-to-Hide," my soul is inviting me to let her make the face of "Letting-Be Hopefully," a face which increasingly has nothing to hide from others or myself. In making her face of "Something-to-Fear," my soul is inviting me to let her make the faces of "Letting-Grow Lovingly" and "Letting-Flow Gracefully" and to let all of these "Good News" faces keep flowing together freely through whatever I fear and am called to face. I find that the soul loves to keep making faces, especially her "Good News" ones.

I find that the only way I can allow my soul to change her "Bad News" faces into "Good News" faces is by turning around and heading in a new direction again and again. That's what I now experience the soul's journey into freedom, and the process of spiritual direction, to really be all about. They're about discerning what face the soul is making and turning in the direction that her "Good News" face suggests. If the soul began giving out T-shirts at this illuminating point in the journey, the message on them all would probably carry the mantra, "Turn, Turn, Turn" and suggest a song that I know all too well.

I can still remember the day the symbol of the faces of the soul first came to me. I was staying in the retreat section of the beautiful old Mission in Santa Barbara, working on the last part of a book on the creative art of living the integrating journey of *Passingover* in a broken world. In it I was attempting to pull together my own experience of the spiritual journey, the many celebrations of Holy Week I had led, and the many courses and retreats I had given on the Process of *Passingover*. I was very pleased and energized by what I was discovering as I wrote and by how well the writing was going.

One day, on my afternoon walk through the downtown area, I entered the courtyard of a beautiful public building that was built in the classical Spanish style. I was immediately drawn to a very large fountain that was in the center of the courtyard. It stood there gracefully transforming the bright afternoon sunlight into flowing gold.

As I walked around the fountain, I admired the sculptures of four human faces through which the water was flowing. Each face was unique and was pointing in a different cardinal direction so that I couldn't see all the faces at once. I had to keep walking around the fountain, moving from face to face.

Then it hit me. "These fountain faces with living water flowing through them are like faces of the soul!" This insight gave me the topic and the central image for the next chapter of my book. The chapter would be on the creative journey from slavery into freedom and how the soul's face keeps changing along the way. I could hardly wait to get back to my room and get started writing it.

By that time I had already left the classroom and was dedicating myself primarily to doing spiritual direction and leading retreats and workshops in discernment. What I began to find was that my growing familiarity with the ever-changing faces of my own soul gave me an inner sensitivity to the changing faces of other persons' souls as well. While others would be sharing their spiritual journey with me or some of the difficulties they were experiencing along the way, it was as though I could feel their soul beginning to make one of her many familiar faces underneath all that my companions were saying. Sometimes it was something like the face they were wearing on the outside. At other times, it was very different. In either case, it gave me a felt sense of where my spiritual companion was in the journey and of what direction they were heading in. This helped me to speak with them from within the way their soul was moving. It also let me recognize when they were trying to live their life with only one very frozen face just as I have on so many occasions.

Of course, in giving retreats and in spiritual direction, I seldom if ever mention the image of the faces of the soul. In my experience that doesn't help others much in the inner work they have to do. Part of that work is discovering for themselves their own inner images of the movement of their soul. But, as often is the case, what helps me personally in being faithful to my own journey often proves helpful in my ministry of spiritually companioning others.

Recently, my soul has been letting me get to know her through the image of her dwelling place. I'm just beginning to realize how, for much of my life, I've been moving both alone and together with other pilgrims from room to room of the soul's dwelling place. As I look back at the spiritual seeking and guiding I've been doing over the past thirty years, it's as if I see a host of pilgrim footprints, including mine. I see these pilgrim footprints tracing the basic shape of the soul's dwelling place and marking the meditative pathway through which we recurrently become more at home in it. These days the image of the soul's dwelling place has become one of my most helpful channels for getting to know my soul. How I see the image of the soul's dwelling place is quite different from the way Teresa of Avila imagined it, but the image itself is proving just as helpful to me as it was for her. It gives me a felt sense of what the soul likes to do, where she likes to do it, the unique atmosphere that her doing it gives to that place, and the sequence in which she usually leads me from room to room of her dwelling place so that I can feel more at home living there.

My priest-scientist brother Joe once told me, with the excitement of the brain physiologist that he was, that the human brain was the last unexplored continent. I was fascinated by that thought and by the great enthusiasm he showed in sharing it. As the inner empiricist I have since become I would now add to that another "unexplored continent"—the soul's dwelling place. But the soul's dwelling place is not merely a continent. I experience it as an unimaginably vast cosmos whose beauty invites each of us to explore it on our own. It's not just a single dwelling place, either. It's a whole cosmos of nested dwelling places in which the inner facts of my life, my true identity and my ultimate destiny reside. As I continue to explore this inner and outer cosmos, I find that it just keeps expanding. There seems to be no end to it. This is where my image of the dwelling place begins to fade out, even when I'm thinking of the biggest, most extraordinarily beautiful mansion I can imagine. The soul's dwelling place is far beyond that. Teresa of Avila puts it nicely when she speaks of "a million dwelling places" and adds, "I don't find anything comparable to the magnificent beauty of a soul and its marvelous capacity. Indeed, our intellects, however keen, can hardly comprehend it, just as they cannot comprehend God; but He Himself says that He created us in His own image and likeness" (*Interior Castle* I: 1). I wholeheartedly agree.

I have the same experience with my image of the soul's dwelling place that I had with my image of her many faces. The more I personally experience the shape, character, and especially the pathway of the soul's movement through her dwelling places, the more I find the image of the soul's dwelling place helping, deepening, and clarifying the ministry I have of spiritually companioning others. I keep the image to myself but as we're journeying together, it lets me feel us moving quite naturally from room to room. I often feel that we're not alone in making this journey, either. It's as though we're being accompanied by a third presence. It's as though the soul is leading us.

These days, the area of the soul's dwelling place that is expanding in an intense way for me is what I call the soul's cloister garden. I initially visualized this area as a very peaceful space at the center of all the soul's dwelling places. I experienced all the other dwelling places to be surrounding it and opening into it. I initially considered the soul's cloister garden to be her central dwelling place where, after a long inward journey, religions, philosophers, theologians, artists, saints, sages, poets and mystics of all traditions can meet inwardly and share what life is really all about at its deepest level. I saw this area to be the soul's place of deepest communing and shared wisdom. It was the deep meeting place.

I'm now seeing that the soul's cloister area is not just one dwelling place, as I had first imagined it to be. It's more like three dwelling places nesting within one another and continually expanding so that, even though it's unimaginable, the innermost dwelling places actually contain the outer ones. What I originally thought to be the whole central cloister area, I now see to be the cloister walk that goes around it. It's the place where the soul likes to lead us in communing with the more-than-personal depths of our lives by walking around the inner garden that is in the center of the dwelling place while ritualizing, celebrating, and talking about what we think is going on in the garden.

Meanwhile, all of the talk and ritualizing that goes on in the cloister walk is pointing to the garden of communing in the center of the cloister area. I now see that this garden is the dwelling place of the soul's most intimate spiritual experience. It's a place where we can only go alone and into which we have to go naked, stripped of everything else.

The real conundrum that I'm being led to explore now is how, when the soul begins leading someone into the cloister garden, many of the religious leaders and spiritual teachers in the cloister walk seem to turn on them. These same leaders and teachers are the very ones who, all along, have been pointing to the garden, talking about it, and celebrating it most enthusiastically. But when someone is personally drawn to leave the cloister walk and enter the garden, their companions start warning them against it, forbidding them to go there, and sometimes, if they have the power, severely punishing them for even thinking about entering the garden. This dramatic change of attitude is a very perplexing conundrum. I'm starting to think of it as "the final taboo." It's not the familiar taboo on doing something morally wrong. It seems to be a taboo for going too far spiritually and entering an area that is beyond our own and others' control. It's like a taboo on entering the Holy of Holies. This taboo boggles much more than my mind. It boggles my heart and my spirit, as well. I think that's why my soul is inviting me now to explore this threshold conundrum with all my mind, with all my heart, and with all my soul. It's a most astonishing taboo.

I'm also beginning to see that the soul's most intimate dwelling place of communing is not her cloister walk. It's her hiding place. It's the invisible place at the very center of the cloister garden. It's a dwelling place that the soul dearly treasures. It's a place that's more intimate to her than she is to herself. It's a place of no place. It's so well hidden that it can't be missed. It's nowhere and everywhere. It's a place of eloquent silence, radiant darkness, and learned ignorance that's totally beyond "this" or "that"; or "you" or "me" and all of the apparent contradictions of our "either/or" way of thinking. It's a place that we can't fully understand or describe. We can only babble about it, just as I'm doing now and point to it through a veil darkly by limping signs and symbols. We can only go around like pilgrims spreading what is a most puzzling rumor about the garden and the hiding place of the soul everywhere we can, in hope that someone might be touched by our babbling, and begin the long journey home to see for themselves.

23

Becoming a Hermit without a Permit

> *Don't tell anybody you're a hermit.*
> —Thomas Merton

As a misfit I guess it's only natural that I spend a lot of time alone. Solitude just comes with the turf and I'm glad. I'm very fond of solitude. It also comes with being dedicated to the intellectual life. Of all the solitary times I've known—and I've known an awful lot of them—I still count my four years studying in Paris as one of the most solitary times in my life.

My real problem with spending a lot of time alone didn't come primarily from me. It came from my fellow Norbertines. They didn't seem to mind when I was mostly alone overseas for eight years. They figured I was studying and writing my dissertation. They didn't mind when I spent more than half of my life alone in my room. They figured I was preparing my college classes or my homilies. They didn't mind too much when I spent an awful long time in the woods on the golf course, either. Given my wayward drives, they figured I was looking for my golf ball. They didn't even mind when I lived apart from the community at the Emmaus house of prayer for eight years. They figured I was busy giving retreats and helping young men discern whether or not God was calling them to become part of our Norbertine community.

When my brothers really began getting upset was when I blew my cover. After getting the Abbot's permission, I built a hermitage in a remote place on the Abbey grounds and began openly telling my brothers that I felt God was calling me to live a more solitary life as a Norbertine priest. That's when I started getting in more trouble, and for a longer period of time, than I ever could have imagined. So I took the line of least resistance. I got permission to spend a year living the contemplative life of the Camaldolese hermits in Big Sur to discern whether or not I was being called to leave the Norbertine community and become one of them.

I don't think our Abbey community would have had any trouble with the way I was going if we had been together in the twelfth century at the Abbey of Prémontré where we were founded. At that time, people all over Europe were having a tough time figuring out who we were. We were starting to look like a bunch of misfits. We weren't fitting into the customary categories of religious life at all. We were priests, or canons, living and dressing as Augustinian lay monks of the strict observance, continuing to preach and minister as priests, and spiritually animating a whole French town and the wider Church throughout Europe as our community continued to grow like Gospel wildfire. What's more, we were founded by a converted nobleman, the many faces of whose life included monk-hermit-canon regular-reformer manqué-wandering preacher-mediator-monastic founder-missionary and archbishop-advisor to the Emperor. The problem we were discussing in the 1960s of "the hyphenated priest"—such as whether or not it was right to be a worker-priest, or a priest-teacher, or priest-scientist—pales in comparison with the richly hyphenated lives our early confreres were living.

So what's the problem? As I have experienced it, the problem is that the intervening eight centuries have let us get organized by "freezing" one of the many archetypal faces that animated and enriched the early creative development of our religious community. That isn't only true of the Order of Prémontré, either. It's true of a very large segment of religious communities at this time. Institutionally "freezing" a community's face seems to be an important part of getting organized and fitting in. As a result, many religious communities may be dying, not from hardening of the arteries, but from hardening of the categories that leaves them with one frozen face. So now, at least theoretically, *either* you're a priest *or* a monk; a cleric *or* a lay person; a minister *or* a contemplative; a community member *or* a solitary; a priest *or* a hermit. The litany goes on and on and the point of it is that *both-and* isn't possible. I think this *either/or* perspective accounts for a big part of the problem

I was facing in pursuing a more solitary way of life in our community of very active priests. My writing a series of essays in which I tried to document, suggest, and defend another point of view from within our own tradition didn't solve the problem, either. I eventually realized that I wasn't being called to give a course on the importance of living as a solitary. I was being called to *live* as a solitary.

When I first returned to the Abbey from my year of discernment with the Camaldolese hermits, I remember a woman asking me where I had been.

"I spent last year living with a community of hermits," I replied.

"There can't be a community of hermits," she commented.

"You know," I suggested, "you really should tell that to the guys I was living with last year. These monks and their confreres have been living as a community of hermits since the eleventh century."

I don't know what she made of that. It must have boggled her mind.

A more immediate problem I was facing at the time was the fallout from "blowing my cover." As long as I could justify a more solitary way of life by the highly visible ministry I was doing, there didn't seem to be any problem. Then I ruined all of that by intentionally "blowing my cover." I trace taking this step to a retreat I made with a wise man of very few words. He was a Cistercian monk who had just finished living for five years in the "Grand Silence" of a Carthusian community of hermits. I was describing my calling to solitude to him and how I had been able to realize it to a degree by keeping it under my hat and maintaining a good ministerial "cover."

He looked straight at me and said, "No cover." I think that was it. It was also when things began getting surprisingly thorny for me. At the end of our retreat, though, he added, "You will find the place God has prepared for you." I was greatly consoled to hear that.

I wish I had known one of my favorite quotations from Thomas Merton at that time. It would have been very helpful. But I didn't come across it until much later. Merton wrote something like, "Don't tell anyone that you're a hermit. Everyone knows what it means to be a hermit except the hermit. That's why he becomes a hermit. To find out what it means to be a hermit."

And there I was, naively trying to make the case for my being "a hermit of Prémontré." I should really have known better, too. I had learned years before, that in order to negotiate a transition as gracefully as possible, it's important to find a word for it with which others are comfortable. "Hermit" was not that kind of word. It can be a big red flag for all kinds of people, especially religious. It can sound like a fancy way of saying "misfit."

As it turned out, the golden word for me in transitioning more gracefully into a simpler and more solitary way of life was "retirement." That's really not an uncommon word, but it took me almost fifteen years to discover it. Actually, I have the Abbot to thank for giving me that word. It was like a golden apple on a plate of silver. Once, as he was listening patiently to me trying to describe my call, my plight, and my plans to him, he said, "It seems to me that what you're talking about, Fran, is being fully retired."

"Fully retired!" With that password, all the doors that seemed to be tightly closed began opening as if by themselves, except of course for the one marked "priests can't retire."

When I looked at our Constitutions I found this description: "A fully retired confrèrè is an emeritus member of the community with no communal or ministerial obligations except to pray for the welfare of the community." What a great description this was of at least part of what "hermit" was beginning to mean to me. And there it was in black and white right in the Constitutions of the Order of Prémontré! So, from then on, I took "fully retired" as my password and quietly tucked "hermit" in a special place in my heart right next to "misfit."

I can't honestly say when I first met Lady Solitude, but the longer I walked with her the more I desired to live with her and the more intense our relationship became. As I soon discovered, walking with her wherever she went is what our relationship is really all about, even though I initially thought that it *should* be about settling down with her in one place for the rest of my life. In relating to her, I've discovered that Lady Solitude has a great deal of the pilgrim in her. It's part of her disarming charm. It's reflected in the eight hermitages we've shared over the past twenty years. And that's not even counting our more-than-annual solitary retreats at monasteries, ashrams, contemplative centers, and other hermitages all over the country. At least in my case, for Lady Solitude, settling down isn't primarily a matter of geography. It's primarily a matter of soul.

I can already hear someone telling me "But you can't be a hermit *and* a pilgrim." My experience has taught me otherwise.

Actually, from time to time, I enjoy just saying to myself the names of the primary hermitages I have shared with Lady Solitude over the past thirty years. These names are now treasured symbols for me of the movement of my spiritual journey and of the very rich times and places I have visited and loved along the way. They are the primary stepping stones of my pilgrimage with Lady Solitude.

Along the way from hermitage to hermitage, it was as though Lady Solitude was teaching me how to walk in the sandals of my twelfth-century Norbertine brothers. She was letting me experience not only their community-hermit faces, but their penitent-retreat-ant-priest-monk-hermit-pilgrim-poet-prophet-preacher-witness-minister-misfit faces as well. For her, the pilgrimage we were making together was not about taking one classic spiritual face and freezing it. It was about learning how, with creative fidelity, to make all the spiritual faces that reflect the soul's inner movement into God. To some, that may not seem to be a proper thing for her to do, but Lady Solitude has a mind of her own. In our relationship, she loves to make faces and to play "making faces" with me, even if many of the faces she makes puzzle me at the time. She not only has a high tolerance for my very hyphenated life, she's largely responsible for it. She actually seems to delight in it.

Whenever I would get settled in one of these hermitages I would begin wondering whether I had finally found "the place God has prepared for me" as my hermit friend had promised I would. For a while, I may even have thought that, finally, this was the place I had been looking for all along. Then, for some reason or other, Lady Solitude would put on her sandals and I'd say to myself, sometimes with great regret, "Oh well, here we go again." There never was any question in my mind, though, whether or not I should go with her. We are meant to be together, no matter where that leads. That much I know.

As important as it is, how to walk in a contemporary way in the sandals of my twelfth century brothers and many other solitary souls is not the only thing that Lady Solitude is teaching me on our pilgrimage together. Among the many things she continues to teach me is that she treasures living in the freedom of the Spirit without most of the traditional religious and social constraints. Another is that she is no recluse. She loves to make a qualitative difference in the world through meditation, heart-to-heart conversation, and creative service. She keeps showing me creative ways in which meditation-ministry and hermit-priest feed into one another for me and for most of the solitaries I know. I experience them as two poles of a creative cycle. Without one of them for any length of time, both of them shrivel up. The same is true for solitude-community, or hermit-monk. For me, isolating one of them dries up the well of creativity. In my case, Lady Solitude is not at all interested in trying to live with only one face. She's willing to live with as many faces as it requires to experience and witness to a deeper, freer, more intense, more creative, and more universal way of communing. That seems to be going much farther than many of our traditional social and religious structures can currently manage or embrace.

When I was first following Lady Solitude all around in order to try to find out for myself what it means to be a hermit, I had no idea that she was preparing me for a new ministry. Now, as I live in full retirement at the Norbertine Hermitage Retreat in New Mexico and welcome other "hermits without permits" to share the simple silence, solitude, and beauty of the desert with me, I marvel at how Lady Solitude has arranged all of this.

Although they're more than welcome here, our Norbertine Hermitage Retreat is not meant to be a place only for official, card-carrying, lifetime hermits. It's a place for part-time, anonymous, "hermits without permits." It's a place where anyone of any faith tradition or with no religious affiliation at all can come when they feel the need to be alone or to speak heart-to-heart with someone, especially themselves or God. It's a place where they can catch their breath; or rest up; or settle down; or pray their way though a problem; or get off the treadmill; or write a book; or ask God for help; or discern which way their life wants to go next. It's a place where they can discover for themselves what it really means for them to be a hermit, at least for a few days.

Since, for as long as they're here, our guests are "hermits without permits," what they do here is nobody else's business. If they want to talk to somebody about it, we're here. If they want to join our community for prayer or Eucharist, we're here. If they simply want us to let them be, that's fine with us, too. That's probably the most important thing we do around here. We let others *be*. As I know from experience, that's when Lady Solitude likes to show up and introduce herself. Mother Nature usually tags along with her, too, since they're the two resident spiritual directors here and, besides, they're very close friends.

There's not much to the Norbertine Hermitage Retreat: a small adobe meditation chapel, five little hermitages, and a simple six-room guesthouse. But, as I experience it, this is an extremely important place for persons who have so little privacy and quietness in their lives that they no longer know who they are. It's an extremely important place for persons who live in a culture that is changing so radically, and at such a bewildering speed, that they just can't keep up. This is a place of Sabbath; of Shalom; of silence and solitude; of soul-searching; of spiritual deepening; and of the kind of personal transformation that can have the most creative social, communal, and religious implications. That's true, even though everyone else in the world knows that hermits can't be a part of that kind of thing. The Norbertine Hermitage Retreat is an *in-between* kind of place in which I feel very much at home. For me, it's a great blessing to be here.

If one of our "hermits without permits" would ever ask me for a word of advice, I wouldn't even have to think twice about it. I'd say right away, "Don't tell anyone you're a hermit. Just be one."

24

Playing Hide-and-Seek with God

> *"He made from one the whole human race*
> *to dwell on the entire surface of the earth,*
> *and he fixed the ordered seasons*
> *and the boundaries of their regions,*
> *so that people might seek God*
> *even perhaps grope for him and find him,*
> *though indeed he is not far from any one of us.*
> *For 'In him we live and move and have our being,'*
> *as even some of your poets have said,*
> *'For we too are his offspring.'"*
>
> —Acts 17: 26-27

*A*fter spending three-quarters of a century seeking God, I'm beginning to think that God loves to play hide-and-seek. I'm also beginning to think that God's very good at it.

I'm not complaining, just stating a fact. I know that's how long I've been seeking God, but I have no idea how long God has been playing hide-and-seek. If it's even half as long as I suspect, it makes me feel as though I haven't even begun to play and that the chances of God not finding me are pretty thin.

As a child, hide-and-seek was one of my favorite games. I can still remember playing it in the street with my little friends in the gathering darkness of a fall evening. The seeker would count loudly from one to ten as the rest of us scampered into the twilight, heading for our hiding places. Then, after a pregnant pause, we would hear the cry, "Ready or not, here I come," and the titillating search was on.

I remember well what a thrill it was to find one of my friends. We would both scream with delight. I can also remember what a thrill it was to be *found* by one of my friends.

I can understand why *I* would scream with delight at finding a friend who was trying to hide from me, but I still have a hard time understanding why in the world I would scream with delight when my friend found *me*. It seems to me that the whole point of the game of hide-and-seek is to hide so well that you can't be found. Being found was like losing. I can't see how that could be any fun. Why in the world would I scream with delight at losing?

I guess that, as a little child, I didn't know any better. I hadn't yet learned that being found shouldn't be any fun because it makes you a loser and nobody likes to be a loser. Since I didn't know that, it really made no difference to me at all whether I found someone else or someone else found me. In either case, I screamed with delight. Maybe, as a child, I thought that in the end, hide-and-seek is really all about screaming with delight.

Maybe that's why I loved to play hide-and-seek so much. I would just keep on playing without even realizing how late and how dark it was getting to be until I heard my mother's voice counting from one to ten. Then I'd run home and continue playing hide-and-seek in my dreams.

If I read the Scriptures right, I can't really blame God for starting this game. In the beginning, God wasn't into hiding at all. As the day came to an end God used to like to take a walk in the garden with us right out in the open. It was my good friends Eve and Adam who really invented hide-and-seek. As far as I know, they are the first ones to hide from God because they discovered they didn't have a thing to wear.

As a little child, not having a thing to wear never seemed to bother me. I don't think it ever really bothered God, either. It seems to me that, deep down, God really doesn't have a thing to wear anyway and could care less. I wouldn't be surprised at all if, in the beginning, God used to show up stark naked for the evening walks with Eve and Adam. So I'm no longer surprised when God still shows up "naked" for the most intimate twilight walks we take together in the garden. So do I. Sometimes, we even "scream with delight" when we find one another this way and see how much we look alike.

So it seems that Eve and Adam invented the game of hide-and-seek all by themselves when they started building a wardrobe so that they could hide themselves from God and from one another. It's hard to tell where they got this idea. Somewhere along the line they must have looked at one another standing there naked and, all of a sudden, decided that they were too exposed. They already knew that they were made in the image and likeness of God but there they were, looking at one another and thinking that they were too exposed. So they started building a wardrobe.

God's reaction to this seems to have been that three can play this game. And when God starts building a wardrobe, look out! It's really impressive. It's beyond anything I can imagine. I know that no wardrobe I've ever built even comes close to it. That doesn't keep me from building a wardrobe, though. I wonder if Eve and Adam had any idea what they started by thinking that they were unfit to be seen.

I've learned an awful lot over the years by playing hide-and-seek with God. For one thing, I've learned that when God calls out, "Francis, where are you? Where are you?" God's not trying to find out where I am. God knows exactly where I am. For God, this whole thing's just a game. As God looks at it, all my hideouts are transparent. So is my whole wardrobe. So am I, for that matter. I sometimes wonder why I still insist on getting all dressed up.

So, right from the start, God and I are playing hide-and-seek on a very uneven playing field. I can get so wrapped up in the game, though, that I forget this from time to time. Then something always happens to remind me how uneven the playing field really is.

So, if God already knows where I am, why does God keep calling out, "Francis, where are you? Where are you?" I had to keep playing hide-and-seek for a long time before I discovered that God keeps calling out like this to remind me that this is just a game that we're playing and that I've hidden myself so well that I've forgotten where I am. When I finally get the message, God can take a break. Then, without hardly realizing it, I take over asking *myself*, "Francis, where are you? Where are you?" That's another thing God is very good at—leaving haunting questions lying around.

No matter how often God and I go through this little dance I'm still always surprised when I hear God's haunting question echoing through me in my own voice. "Francis, where are you? Francis, where are you?" It's like catching myself humming a tune I never liked and wondering where in the world that song came from and how in the world I started humming it.

By passing this "Where are you?" melody on to me, God subtly changes the name of the game. Instead of hiding, I now begin seeking where I'm hiding so that I can tell myself and God where I am. This can get very complicated. I can never do it without taking off at least one layer of what I've been hiding under. I often do this with great reluctance and very slowly so that I can admire the amount of work I put into weaving or borrowing this particular garment. It's been part of the very imaginative wardrobe that I've been painstakingly creating for a long time. But God's disrobing question makes this particular garment transparent to me now, so why should I keep wearing it? So I take it off and let it go and, at least for the time being, discover where I've been hiding. I'm reluctant to admit it but as I take something off like this, I sometimes even scream with childlike delight just as I would when I'd find one of my little friends who was trying to hide from me.

But, from time to time, I find that I've had enough of all of this. Then I try to get off the hook and not let God change the name of the game on me anymore. So, when God calls out, "Francis, where are you? Where are you?" I answer right back, "Don't come near me, I'm naked!" even though I know full well that I'm very well dressed. Then God cuts right through my reply by asking, "Who told you that you were naked?" Hoping to get God to back off, I angrily counter with, "Who do you think you're talking to? Do you think somebody has to tell *me* that I'm naked? *Nobody* told me. I can see that for myself!"

"I thought so," God whispers, and then goes into hiding again.

"I thought so?" I start puzzling, "I thought so?" What does God mean by that? That's how God hooks me once again with one of those haunting questions and changes the name of the game on me. Then, after counting very slowly to ten, I start seeking out where I'm hiding. What else can I do?

Over time, playing hide-and-seek with God has also taught me that, whether I like it or not, I like the layered look in life. Dressing up that way gives me a lot of hiding places to fall back on even if I have to let one or two of them go from time to time. I may like to pretend that I'm walking naked with God again when I take off my overcoat but, deep down, I know full well that a lot more has to go if I'm really going to be walking naked with God again. I know I like the layered look but it always surprises me how many layers I'm wearing and how extensive my self-made wardrobe actually is. It even begins to feel embarrassing. Fashion is one thing, but this is something else.

I used to wonder what God was doing during the break God would take after changing the name of the game on me and leaving me playing hide-and-seek with myself. At first, I thought that God must have gone into hiding. After going back again and again to playing hide-and-seek with God, I knew *for sure* that God went into hiding. But I had to do an awful lot more seeking to discover just how good God really is at hiding. God's a real master at it. I started to realize this when I began to notice the difference between how God hides and how I hide. I hide *behind* things and persons and *under* tightly-knit layers of rational and emotional clothing. And I hide in the most remote and secret places I can find.

I find that God doesn't hide in this way at all. Unlike me, God doesn't hide *behind* and *under* things and persons. God hides *within* and *beyond* things and persons. I haven't taken the full inventory yet, but after all of my seeking, I'm beginning to find God hiding *within* and *beyond* every single thing and every single person in all of creation—including me! I'm talking about a real pro at hiding!

Also, unlike me, God doesn't hide in the most remote and secret places. I keep finding God hiding in places that are so easy for me to overlook simply because they're so obvious. They're right under my nose.

That's the way God keeps fooling me—by hiding out in plain sight. That's the last place I'd think of looking. You'd think that, after a while, I'd catch on to this, but I don't. I still go around looking for God in the most remote and secret places. It isn't as though I haven't heard about God's strange way of hiding before:

> *...though indeed he is not far from any one of us.*
> *For 'In him we live and move and have our being,'*
> *as even some of your poets have said,*
> *'For we too are his offspring.'*

But that doesn't seem to make any difference. It's one thing for me to hear about God's unbelievably obvious hiding places, and it's something else entirely for me personally to discover that for myself, one person and one thing at a time. It seems to me that God and I will be playing hide-and-seek and screaming for delight for a very long time.

What has helped me a lot in discovering God's hiding places is the intense meditative work I've been doing in exploring my soul's dwelling place. Most of the time, I have to take off a layer or two of clothing at the threshold before entering one of my soul's many dwelling places. Then, as my meditative writing deepens, I begin finding God hiding all over the place. Discovering this teaches me to honor every aspect of my life and to treat it with mindful reverence because God may be hiding there. When I actually find God hiding right there in the middle of my own experience I feel that, at long last, I'm beginning to get the hang of what playing hide-and-seek with God is really all about.

This experience isn't limited to when I'm doing my inner meditative work, though. It overflows gracefully into my soul's outward dwelling places of the porch and the marketplace as well. Then I begin finding God hiding everywhere, in every person and every thing. This greatly expands the playing field of my game of hide-and-seek with God. There is no limit to this playing field--God's hiding all over the place, and even in no place at all.

About five or six years ago the level of my play took another quantum leap. As part of our work in meditative writing we read back aloud to ourselves what we have written in order to deepen and expand the scope of our inner sensitivity and experience. One day, as I was listening to retreatants reading aloud, all of a sudden it hit me—"This is *lectio divina. It's holy reading!*" As we read aloud what we've written, we're meditatively reading and honoring the scriptures of our own lived experience."

After this, I began to realize that there's a much overlooked Fifth Gospel in which God also hides. I began to find God hiding, not only in the Gospels according to Matthew, Mark, Luke and John, but also in the Good News according to me—and every other person as well. At this point in the game, I began to see every single person's life as a Fifth Gospel, as one of God's many surprising hiding places.

Discovering another person's life as well as my own being a kind of Fifth Gospel has been a breakthrough for me. It often overflows into how I search the Holy Scripture and how I look at and listen to my own and other persons' lives. It lets me see that the four Gospels are not just about the life of Jesus Christ. In every single thing they say, they are all about *my* life and the life of every single person and community who reads them as part of their ongoing game of hide-and-seek with God. Angelus Silesius, a celebrated Christian mystic of the seventeenth century, seems to be speaking from a similar discovery when he writes:

> *Christ could be born a thousand times in Galilee—*
> *but all in vain until he is born in me.*

This experience of my life as a Fifth Gospel brings some very dear and treasured texts from the other four Gospels alive in me in a deeply personal way. I never thought of them before as speaking about me, but now I know that they do. This makes them so filled with Life and Mystery that I hardly dare to read them aloud. When I hear them speaking about me, these familiar texts are among the most unlikely places in which I find God and I hiding-seeking-finding one another.

"Whose image is this?"
"The Kingdom of God is within you."
"In God we live and move and have our being."
"I live now, not I, but Christ lives in me."
"You are the body of Christ."
"Your life is hidden with Christ in God."
"You are my Beloved Son."
"The Father and I are One."
"So that they may all be one,
as you, Father, are in me and I in you,
that they also may be in us."

As I experience these and so many other of my treasured scripture texts speaking about me, I begin to discover how God and I have been hiding together in them all along, and I didn't even know it. That doesn't usually make me scream with delight, though. It just lets a quiet delight settle over me as it leads me into an eloquent silence and invites me to take off anything and everything that could come between my God and me, so that there's nothing between us now. There's nothing between us now—absolutely nothing.

As I've been doing that, three things are becoming clear to me that, at least from my side, are radically transforming the game of hide-and-seek that I've been playing with God. First, playing hide-and-seek is not a game of cat-and-mouse for God as it often is for me. It's not just an amusing pass time but actually God's basic way of loving me. Realizing this has completely changed the name of the game for me. It has given it a new urgency and has put a whole new thrill in it. It has also let me see what's behind all of the screaming with delight that God and I keep doing. This has been a delightful revelation to me.

Another thing that I'm seeing more clearly than ever before is that, at least as far as I'm concerned, God's favorite hiding place is me. While I've been running around for so long trying to find God, all the time God has been hiding within me and quietly smiling at me. This is the most unlikely hiding place; I've been overlooking it all along. It's also an inspired hiding place—I'd never think of looking for God there. It's so close to me that I can't even see it. Talk about hiding right under my nose! Discovering God's favorite hiding place is changing my whole experience of playing hide-and-seek with God. It's also making me suspect that, from now on, there's going to be a lot more screaming with delight going on between us.

Together with these two experiences, I'm finally beginning to discover my own favorite hiding place—it's God. There's no doubt about it. I may have thought before that God would never think of looking for me there. But now I know that God is *always* looking for me there. So here we are, God hiding in me and me hiding in God so that we can't tell one from the other. Who would ever think of looking for us there? Maybe this, as the hermit once promised, is the place God has prepared for me.

While I can feebly point to this hiding place, there's no way in the world that I can describe what I experience when I'm hiding in it. However, it begins to feel like what I believe it must feel like to be in the soul's hiding place at the center of her cloister garden. It begins to feel like the place-of-no-place that is the no-place-of-every-place: God hiding in me and me hiding in God. It's a more intimate place than I will ever be able to imagine. It's not only a place of God loving me and me loving God, it's a place of God loving God. From there, one by one, all of God's hiding places are becoming transparent to me.

When I start babbling like this, I know that I'm not making any sense anymore, even to me. I also know that, even if I can't fully express it, this is how it really is with me. But when I hear myself babbling like this I now know that it's time to be still and to return to the hiding place from which all of this babbling comes,

In the Silence...
in the Silence...

25

A Timely Death

*Why wait to die
until the very last minute,
and have to go elsewhere
for the rest of our life?*

*Why not die early,
like the Prophet,
in the middle of his years,
or the Messiah,
in the vigor of his youth?*

*Then we could stay around for a while,
living our life from the Easter side,
coming and going as a graceful breeze,
like those who walk on the wind
and leave no footprints.*

*What a difference that would make
in how we live.*

*What a difference that would make
in how we die.*
   —Last Night I Died

*I*n my fifty years as a priest I've presided at the burial of many faithful Christians. In doing so, I've heard more people say, "What an untimely death" than I care to remember. I've heard it said so often that I even have a recurrent fantasy about it.

As we're receiving the body of the deceased at the church door, a man turns to me and sadly says, "What an untimely death."

"Wasn't she a hundred and five years old?" I whisper.

"Yes, she was" he says, shaking his head. "What an untimely death."

"Gee," I think to myself, "I wonder how old you have to be to have a timely death?"

But I did experience my brother Joe's sudden death to be a timely one. Not for *him*, of course, but for *me*. Joe was only fifty-four years old and just starting to turn all the energy, study, and scientific research he had invested in experimental psychology toward focusing on the soul's journey into God. I was eagerly waiting to see what would come from his turning in that direction and what we might be able to do together along those lines. Then Joe died. What a most "untimely death."

As it resonated in my own life, however, Joe's death was, and continues to be, a timely death. It made me question and reevaluate the frantically over-extended priestly life I was living. It was as though much of that life died, or began to die, with Joe's death. One by one, many of the things I'd been investing my whole life in lined up to be meditatively looked at against the horizon of eternity and of my newly-discovered finite energy. Thanks to Joe's death, this became the critically important agenda that I took with me into the rest of my sabbatical year of transitioning from the classroom to God knows what. Without thinking of it in this way at the time, it was as though, as Joe died, he handed me the torch he had been carrying so faithfully and pointed me in the direction I should go. As things unfolded, I found myself exploring, in whatever way I could, the deep connection between psychology and spirituality—between the university and the monastery—on the soul's spiritual journey into God. My friendship with Ira Progoff and, through him, with C. G. Jung's work, was immensely helpful to me in doing this. So there I was, running on the narrow track of the in-between again and lighting the way with the torch Joe had passed me thanks to his most "timely death."

I can hear Joe chiming in now...

"You know, Fran, I see my death as a timely death, too. My first heart

attack let me know for sure that I had only two or three years to live. How many people get that kind of advance notice? I considered it a special blessing.

And, as you know, even though I gave it all I had and more, I never was that attached to this life. Although I really loved it and marveled at it all my life, for me, it was always pointing to a very different quality of life that I would find on the other side of dying. If that didn't take away any fear I may have had of dying, my near-death experience in the operating room certainly did. I felt that it actually gave me a foretaste of what dying was really like. How many people get a gift like that?

My near-death experience also let me decide for myself whether my death would be timely or not at that moment. That still seems like a great grace to me. At the time, I didn't know why I felt that it would have been untimely for me to die from my first heart attack, but now I can see why. The two additional years that God gave me were like a completely new lease on life for me. They let me live with a greater ease and freedom than I had ever been able to do before. It was as though I had died and that the life I was living now wasn't my own. That let me relate to others with the fullness of love that I had been carrying around within me for most of my life but didn't quite know how to express. Those two extra years also let me pass the torch of priesthood and of the search for Wisdom to you as carefully as I could. I was happy to be able to do that. Finally, to be allowed to die while celebrating the power of God's Word and of the Eucharist with my brothers, friends, and students at the College—as a priest I couldn't have asked for a more timely death. What a gift.

So mine was a very timely death, Fran, even for me."

As I think of it now, Joe's death wasn't only a timely death for me. It was also a sort of near-death experience as were all the major transitions I've gone through in my life. They all felt like a kind of dying and then choosing freely to come back to life in the hope of enjoying a new season. They all felt like a rehearsal for rising from the dead.

Leaving home, leaving the country, leaving the classroom, leaving my life and ministry in the Jemez Mountains, leaving my active priestly ministry, leaving my actively communal religious way of living and retiring into solitude—all had this near-death character for me. They all involved a letting-go in trust, not of my life as a whole, but of the specific form my life had taken up until then. They all involved my turning in hope toward unlived possibilities that were beyond the horizon of what I could see or imagine at the time. And, in between, they all involved my walking barefoot, if not completely naked, in deep darkness, feeling my way like a blind man who doesn't know where he's going. They all involved my feeling as though my whole world was falling apart. In a very real way, it was falling apart.

In one way or another, every transformation I've experienced in my life has had this "brushing with death" character about it. That makes me feel as though I've lived many lives, and died many deaths, and have been going around in expanding and deepening spirals of dying and rising all my life.

No wonder I feel like a misfit. All of my experiences of transformation started with my feeling somewhat out of place where I was. They then went on to my feeling *really* out of place where I was. Then I would finally honor that feeling and start to move on, which at least for a while, made me feel even *more* out of place than I did before. As I look at it now, feeling like a misfit was an integral part of the creative movement of my whole spiritual journey.

I wish I could say that, at the time, I found each of these painfully disorienting "brushes with death" to be timely deaths, but I honestly can't say that. As I was going through them, they often felt most *untimely*. That was a big part of how painful they were. It was reflected in the litany I would keep reciting during these times.

"Why this, O Lord?
Why now, O Lord?
Why here, O Lord?
Why me, O Lord?"

The answer to this litany that I sometimes heard coming out of the silence was,

"Why not, O Fran?"

If that was meant to be consoling, it failed dismally. It was bad enough having to go through all of this, without having to argue about it. But, as I remained faithful to the journey that led me through these brushes with death, eventually, all of them gave birth in me to a sense of being given a new lease on life and of being more deeply connected to life's Mystery than I was before.

Then, in retrospect, I would begin to see how timely each of these little deaths actually was and my litany would be transformed from one of lament for the tragedy of it all into one of gratefulness and praise for the wonder of how it all worked out. Of course, this "posthumous" perspective always came a little late, but it still let me wholeheartedly celebrate the event of my own "timely death."

It may have been during one of these times of letting go of it all that I got the inspiration for how the gravestone on my final resting-place should read. Under the customary listing of my name and the dates of birth and death, I envisioned the inscription,

What are the other options?

Of course, there's no chance of my ever actually getting a gravestone like that. A pun like that would be totally out of place in our Abbey cemetery. I wouldn't want to go out on such a sour and long-lasting note as that. But this inscription still rings true to me, even with my tongue tucked firmly in my cheek.

It now rings even more true to me than it did at first. As I've become more experienced in negotiating transitions in my life, especially as they became more and more inward, I've begun to experience the deep truth behind my imagined gravestone inscription. At these spiritual intersections in my life, I didn't really *have* another option. Of course, I was always free to refuse to "let-go trustingly" and to keep clinging to what was or had been, but I knew that would be lethal in an even more deadly way. Regardless of how old I was, I knew that clinging to what was would be a most untimely death for me. If I wanted to be faithful to my unfolding journey, willingly letting-go in trust and seeing what would come of that was the only live option I really had. I knew the spiritual integrity of my life depended on it. "What are the other options?" Indeed.

When I finally did get the chance to inscribe "What are the other options?" on my gravestone, however, I didn't do it. Even though I knew it didn't have the same panache, I inscribed, "F.W.D./EASTER, 1988/R.I.P."

Actually, I didn't inscribe it on an honest-to-goodness gravestone. I inscribed it on the fresh concrete footing that I had poured for the twelve-foot redwood cross that I had built and erected in the garden of Star of the Sea hermitage in Big Sur. I had spent all of the Lenten Season ritually building the cross and pruning the great old oak tree that shaded the hermitage. Then, on Good Friday, I poured the footing and carved my gravestone inscription in the wet cement. As the sun rose on Easter Sunday morning, there the Cross stood, looking in two directions. At one and the same time, it was looking right at me and looking out to sea.

This is the most formally I have ever ritualized one of my transitional "brushes with death." It was a way of celebrating my intention to live the rest of my life much more consciously "from the Easter side."

At the time, I was fifty-four years old and a little more than half way through my year of discernment with the Camaldolese hermits. I had already discerned that I wasn't being called to apply for a "hermit permit" there. I was being called to take what I had learned from living there with me and to live as a wandering "hermit without a permit." So I spent the rest of the year peacefully looking into my self by day and looking out to sea by night from Star of the Sea hermitage, and breathing in the deep solitude, silence, and beauty of that place that I hoped would accompany me wherever I would go.

To my mind, this was a most timely death—and a most timely

rising from the dead, too. It set the spiritual course that my life has been taking ever since. It has also made the New Camaldoli Hermitage and the wilderness of Big Sur one of my most beloved resting places in the world.

FAREWELL

Last night,
I died.

They say it was the leftover pasta.
How can I tell them now
that it was my heart?

And, perhaps,
the marinara sauce?
   —Last Night I Died

I don't think this is much of a poem but I'm very thankful anyway that I stopped the car halfway across the Mojave Desert and wrote it down. That gesture seemed to tap into my "underground poetry well" that had been bone-dry for several years. During the next seven months of retreat at the Hermitage in Big Sur, a flood of poems came pouring out of me. To be exact, one hundred and forty-three of them. What a great reward for honoring just one little drip of a poem in the middle of the desert. Life is very magnanimous.

Actually, I don't think that it was the marinara sauce that did it. I think it was the pressure I was feeling from my last minute preparations for the trip that would begin my "creative retirement." I was leaving in the morning to begin another extended retreat at the Camaldolese Hermitage in Big Sur. And just as my confreres had predicted, I wasn't even half packed.

After dinner, my heart started pounding, my blood pressure shot up, and I began gasping for breath. One of our novices who is a nurse, took my pulse and blood pressure and said that the problem probably was the leftover pasta. It had been around for a few days.

He may have been right, but I took it as my heart's way of anxiously saying goodbye to my former way of life. There were good grounds for that anxiety, too. In moving into full retirement I was experiencing yet another major change of heart and I knew that a challenging change of life wasn't going to be far behind. I knew from experience that it wouldn't make much sense for me to try to tell my brothers about my change of heart. As unlikely as it was, "marinara sauce" was as good a password as any for the change of heart that I knew was going on within me.

In my present life in retirement at the Norbertine Hermitage Retreat in Albuquerque I'm still living from the energy of this retreat of transition that I made many years ago. It's been a long, hard, and often painful journey to work out the details of how I would be able to live creatively in full retirement as a Norbertine priest. There was a lot going against it and many "little deaths" along the way that were multiplied by the fact that I'm a member of a religious community. I was asking a struggling little community in the first phases of its development to trust that my call was the work of the Spirit, to accept me as a misfit, and to mission me, not only as a hermit but also as a hermit without a permit. I was asking an awful lot of my community. So, when it actually happened, I knew for sure that it was the work of the Spirit and so were the several timely deaths that I experienced along the way. Lady Solitude must have been working overtime.

So now I'm living "the quiet life," as my sister Catherine liked to call it. I'm feeling very blessed in being permitted to live in this way, too. I'm experiencing it as a completely new lease on life. This year of double jubilee marks a very graced and creative time in my life. Misfit that I am, I'm celebrating as a hermit without a permit now, in heartfelt praise and thanksgiving as I continue my journey. Hopefully I'll be doing this more carefully than many of the things I did as a younger man and, if God gives me breath, much more peacefully.

MY SONG

*Lord, you are my song.
I have been singing you
my whole life long.*

*But now I have forgotten the words,
and the melody as well,
or have grown out of them.*

*All I can hear is the silent sound
of your breath moving
through the marrow of my bones.*

*I so long to sing my song.
But how can I sing it now,
without the words or music?*

*It's all so strange.
This silent song.
without words, or music.*

*But, for as long as I live,
I will listen to the sound
of your breath moving through me,
and, if it pleases you,
I will be your song.*

www.ingramcontent.com/pod-product-compliance
Lightning Source LLC
Chambersburg PA
CBHW020051170426
43199CB00009B/245